Rachael's
Good Eats

Rachael's Good Eats

EASY, LAID-BACK, NUTRIENT-RICH RECIPES

Rachael DeVaux, RD

Photography by Eva Kolenko

ST. MARTIN'S GRIFFIN
NEW YORK

First published in the United States
by St. Martin's Griffin, an imprint of
St. Martin's Publishing Group

www.stmartins.com

Photography by Eva Kolenko

Designed by Jan Derevjanik

Library of Congress Cataloging-in-
Publication Data

Names: DeVaux, Rachael, author.
Title: Rachael's good eats : easy, laid-back,
nutrient-rich recipes /
    Rachael DeVaux.
Description: First edition. | New York :
St. Martin's Griffin, [2023] |
    Includes index.
Identifiers: LCCN 2022037973 | ISBN
9781250850393 (hardcover) | ISBN
    9781250850409 (ebook)
Subjects: LCSH: Quick and easy cooking. |
LCGFT: Cookbooks
Classification: LCC TX833.5 .D48 2023 |
DDC 641.5/12—dc23/eng/20220817
LC record available at https://lccn.loc.gov/
2022037973

Our books may be purchased in
bulk for promotional, educational,
or business use. Please contact your
local bookseller or the Macmillan
Corporate and Premium Sales
Department at 1-800-221-7945,
extension 5442, or by email at
MacmillanSpecialMarkets@macmillan.com.

First Edition: 2023

10 9 8 7 6 5 4

To Bridger, my sister, and my parents for being my taste testers all these years.

And to my sous chef, Ellie, for being my number one gal in the kitchen.

CONTENTS

Introduction

When I first created my website, Rachael's Good Eats, it was with the intention of combining my two loves: inspiring people to make delicious food that supports their wellness goals and encouraging people to incorporate daily movement into their lives. But more than anything, I wanted to prove that a healthy lifestyle can be enjoyable *and* doable. Just as I wouldn't tell you that you needed to spend hours in the gym slogging through workouts that you despise in order to feel better in your body, I would never tell you that you had to give up all the foods you love, spend tons of time cooking "specialty" meals with hard-to-find ingredients, or sweat it out over every macronutrient. I want to show you just how simple it is to make tasty and nourishing food in your own kitchen, without heaps of cooking experience or fancy appliances.

As a registered dietitian and fitness trainer, I blend living an active life with cooking foods that fuel it. I've spent countless hours learning about the most nutritious ingredients out there and perfecting recipes that put them to good use—so you don't have to. I'm not a chef, but my passion for cooking food for the people I care for—plus using my husband as an expert at-home tester these past ten years—has equipped me with a ton of kitchen know-how.

Want to know the secret to nailing the perfect combination of healthy *and* satisfying? Using *real* ingredients. I love cooking with veggies, good-for-you fats, quality proteins (both animal and plant), and a variety of complex carbohydrates—food that comes in its whole form, not food that comes from a bag or box. I also swap in nutritionally dense ingredients for what I use most, like brain-boosting extra-virgin olive oil in place of inflammatory canola oil, and mineral-rich maple syrup in place of refined cane sugar. So, yes, Orange Chicken and Twix Bars are still on the menu! They might look a little different than they did when you were growing up, but without the excessive amounts of processed sugar and refined carbohydrates, they will actually fuel your body *and* feed your soul.

I started cooking during college, where I studied nutrition and created my Instagram, @rachaelsgoodeats, to share what I was eating every day. Instagram was my passion project. I loved being creative in the kitchen and sharing how to cook knockout meals without many ingredients. Cooking for myself every day also allowed me to discover a few food sensitivities that I was dealing with, and I've been mostly dairy- and gluten-free ever since.

I guarantee you're going to love these recipes—not only for the insane flavor but because balanced meals with real ingredients will add energy to your life. While these dishes are perfect for those of you who are trying to get the most energy for your training, they're also ideal for college students who are trying to cook healthy meals for one (been there!), busy parents trying to get more veggies into their little ones' diet, and anyone else who refuses to believe that healthy cooking can't be absolutely delicious. No matter if your kitchen is a place where you spend a lot of time already or if you're a cooking newbie, I'm here to show you that well-balanced recipes don't need to take hours or a ton of nutritional knowledge. Most of the one-hundred-plus recipes in this book can be made in under thirty minutes, and all of them reflect what I've learned as a dietitian in terms of eating a well-rounded diet. Plus, throughout these coming pages, I'm going to give you plenty of valuable tips and shortcuts for you to keep in mind while you're in the kitchen.

Ultimately, you're going to love what you cook and how you feel when eating these meals—I just know it.

Let's eat!

—Rachael

one

COOKING
THE RGE WAY

My Food Philosophy

Before we get into the recipes, I want to offer some simple tips that you can adopt to live—and maintain—a happy, healthy lifestyle:

Eat for fuel. Nutrients are fuel. I always consider how ingredients are going to benefit my body and help my performance, not just in the gym but throughout the entire day. I want food that's going to make me feel *good*. So good that it allows me to virtually train thousands of people, get great sleep (seven to eight hours), and have enough energy to keep up with my demanding schedule (and my two weenie dogs). I believe that when you start thinking of food as potential energy, your mealtime choices make a positive shift.

Lean in to cooking. This is always my first tip when someone asks about how to eat a more balanced diet. When you're in the kitchen, you're in control of the ingredients you consume, which isn't the case when you eat out or buy packaged food. But no need to jump into the deep end with complicated recipes. Start small and keep it easy! You'll find a ton of super-simple, super-quick recipes in this book to help you out if you're not a fan of being in the kitchen or don't have much experience *yet*. Also, it might sound cheesy, but make cooking fun! Turn on music or a podcast, cook for someone else, buy a pretty serving dish, set the vibe by setting the table, give yourself plenty of time, and get your groceries delivered, if that helps. Making it enjoyable will make it sustainable.

Focus on anti-inflammatory ingredients. I'm big on incorporating ingredients that will play a role in reversing the body's inflammatory process. Inflammation is our body's natural response anytime there's a foreign invader or an injury present. Basically, your body is alerted to aid in the healing process, but sometimes when your genetics, diet, or lifestyle habits continue to ring the alarm (thanks, Bey) even after the threat has passed, chronic inflammation can happen. This can lead to problems like joint pain, bloating, gut issues, psoriasis, diabetes, or other health issues. You'll find a lot of inflammation-controlling ingredients in this book, such as turmeric, berries, nuts, fish, avocado, and extra-virgin olive oil. These foods are staples in my pantry and fridge. They're rich in vitamins, minerals, and other nutrients, like omega-3 fatty acids, magnesium, fiber, and vitamin C.

Limit added sugars. Listen, I know how to make a mean dessert, but I also do my best to be aware of the amount of added sugars in my diet because they're known to be both inflammatory and dehydrating. Eating a diet rich in added sugars—even in something that seems as innocent as your everyday coffee creamer, your favorite granola and fruity yogurt combo, not to mention the sugary condiments you may keep in the fridge—can lead to low energy, weight gain, brain fog, less restful sleep, hormonal imbalance, skin issues, and in some cases, chronic illness. I'm such a firm believer that you can't unlock your best health until you've kicked your dependence on added sugar that

I've developed a Seven-Day Added-Sugar Detox. (To purchase the ebook, visit https://shopgoodeats.com/products /7-day-added-sugar-detox.)

I'm telling you, once you limit sugar consumption for just one week, cravings will diminish, and natural sweets will actually taste *sweeter*. This helps with both sugar cravings and the types of sweets you have a taste for. For example, when I eat less sugar overall, foods like fresh fruit taste super sweet and satisfying, versus when I'm consuming more added sugar than usual and find myself needing a processed food to take the edge off.

Basic is good. Go back to the basics of eating whole foods instead of relying on heavily processed packaged food. I know that processed foods seem like the easy choice (they are!), but I promise you: once you make the shift to eating more real foods (and noticing how they make you feel), the processed stuff gets less appealing. I'll show you how to prep whole foods ahead of time so you always have meals and snacks on hand.

Find a swap. Instead of swearing off certain foods or recipes, I like to get creative. Simple swaps are the key to keeping almost any dish on the healthy-eating menu. I live to remake my childhood favorites into better-for-you staples that my friends and family love. You'll recognize some "dupes" in this cookbook, like Zucchini Lasagna and Thin Mint Chip Smoothie, that taste even better than the "real" versions.

Forget about a one-size-fits-all method. A single way of eating can't meet everyone's needs. Each person is different when it comes to exercise goals, food intolerances (dairy and gluten for me), hormone levels, sleep schedules, physical limitations, etc. If something doesn't work, do you! The info you'll get in this book will empower you to become your best self through improved daily habits. However, knowing that lifestyle changes may be challenging to implement, I suggest you focus on small modifications that will add up over time, like incorporating greens into your lunches and dinners, drinking 75 to 100 ounces of water per day, getting seven to eight hours of sleep every night, and finding some type of movement you love to do daily.

Listen to your body. There's no such thing as one ideal "diet" for everyone, only the one that makes you feel the best. For me, that meant taking note of how things like gluten, refined sugar, and dairy affected my health and adjusting my diet accordingly. For you, the adjustments could look different. I recommend paying close attention to how you feel after eating a meal. Did it make you feel bloated, sluggish, less than ideal? If so, then that meal may have contained a food that isn't great for you personally, even if it's technically "healthy."

TWO-DAY SAMPLE MEAL GUIDE (Without Added Sugar)

Though all the recipes in this book were crafted to make you feel your best, I wanted to include a two-day version of my Added-Sugar Detox to refresh your taste buds and remind you how good it feels to consume more nutrient-dense foods and less added sugar.

I can't wait to hear about your experience sticking to the recipes in this book. Who knows, you might surprise yourself enough to take on the challenge of my full Seven-Day Added-Sugar Detox. Find the entire guide on shopgoodeats.com.

DAY ONE

Breakfast: PB&J Smoothie (pg 54) with Twenty-Minute Paleo Granola (pg 24), omit the maple syrup

Lunch: White Bean Tuna Salad (pg 77)

Snack: Basil Artichoke Hummus (pg 166) with fresh veggies and almond flour crackers or brown rice crackers

Dinner: Goat Cheese–Stuffed Mushrooms (pg 86)

Side: Broccolini with Caramelized Shallots (pg 182)

Dessert: Superfood Chocolate Bark (pg 222)

DAY TWO

Breakfast: Folded Greek Omelet (pg 46)

Lunch: RGE Cobb (pg 66)

Snack: Raw AB&J Bars (pg 144)

Dinner: Baked Crusted Halibut (pg 112)

Sides: Coconut Lime Rice (pg 170), Sesame Broiled Bok Choy (pg 178)

Dessert: Small handful of fresh berries

Kitchen Staples and Must-Haves

The more you cook the recipes in this book, and the more you start replacing some of the processed foods in your diet with healthier ingredients, the more you're going to realize just how amazing you feel. And when that happens, I can assure you that you're never going to want to look back. To help you on a journey to better health, I came up with a list of ingredients—and some kitchen tools—that are helpful to keep on hand so that a delicious, nourishing snack or meal is never more than a few minutes away.

A note on buying organic: Whenever I'm buying anything at the store, I do my best to go with the cleanest item. That usually means organic, and in the case of meat, fish, dairy, and eggs, pasture-raised or wild-caught. Not only does shopping organic mean you're reducing your exposure to harmful pesticides, but you are also retaining more of the beneficial nutrients of the food. You can *taste* the difference. If you're wondering how to spend your grocery dollars wisely, look online for the Clean Fifteen and Dirty Dozen lists, which tell you the produce items that contain the least (Clean Fifteen) and the most (Dirty Dozen) pesticide residue. For instance, berries and spinach are two things I'll always buy organic because they're consistently high on the Dirty Dozen list. New lists are generated every year, so it's a good idea to stay up to date.

Here's just a little look into what I always keep stocked in our kitchen. You can substitute wherever you need to—for example, if you don't have arrowroot starch, pure cornstarch can work. When it comes to cooking sprays, I tend to grab the ones made from avocado oil, extra-virgin olive oil, or coconut oil.

IN THE FRIDGE

Unsweetened nondairy milk: almond, coconut, and cashew

Fresh produce: Broccolini, avocados, bell peppers, cucumbers, asparagus, oranges, lemons, limes, zucchini, berries, mixed greens, fresh ginger

Stone-ground and Dijon mustard

100% pure maple syrup

Poultry: chicken breast, ground chicken, ground turkey, chicken sausage

Pasture-raised eggs

Fish: salmon, halibut, cod

Dairy: You won't find a lot of dairy (aka cow's milk) in this book, because I'm sensitive to casein, which can be the cause of intolerance in a lot of individuals. I've found that goat's milk is much easier to digest, so I've included it in a handful of recipes. Of course, feel free to substitute cow's milk dairy one-to-one if it isn't an issue for you.

Goat's/sheep's milk cheese: feta, sharp cheddar, chèvre

IN THE FREEZER

Organic fruit (especially those that are anti-inflammatory): strawberries, raspberries, blueberries, and blackberries

Peeled bananas for smoothies

Spinach for smoothies

Gluten-free bread

IN THE PANTRY

Flours: almond, gluten-free/paleo, coconut, arrowroot (aka arrowroot starch or powder)

Nut butters (with no added oils or sweeteners)

Raw cacao powder

Cacao nibs

Camu camu

Spirulina

Matcha

Ghee (the lactose has been removed)

Dark chocolate

Raw honey

Coconut sugar

Unsweetened shredded coconut

Dates

Vegan protein powder

Baking soda

Baking powder

CANNED & PACKAGED

Canned cannellini beans

Canned pinto beans

Brown rice pasta (Jovial brand)

Brown rice, basmati rice

Organic whole rolled oats

Crackers: Simple Mills, Mary's, Jilz

Brown rice crackers

Bone broth

SPICES, HERBS & OTHER SEASONINGS

(My spice collection runs deep; these are my must-haves.)

Sea salt

Ground pepper

Garlic powder

Oregano, fresh or dried

Basil, fresh or dried

Rosemary, fresh or dried

Fennel seed

Red chili flakes

Ground cumin

Chili powder

Ground turmeric

Ground cinnamon

Ground Nutmeg

Vanilla extract

Peppermint extract

NUTS & SEEDS

(Buy them raw to give you the most flexibility.)

Walnuts

Pecans

Almonds

Cashews

Hempseeds

Ground flaxseed

Pumpkin seeds

Sunflower seeds

OILS

Extra-virgin olive oil

Avocado oil

Coconut oil

Toasted sesame oil

CONDIMENTS & SAUCES

Coconut aminos

Tamari

Ketchup (I like Primal Kitchen)

Teriyaki sauce (I like Primal Kitchen)

Enchilada sauce (I like Siete)

VINEGARS

Apple cider vinegar

Balsamic vinegar

Red wine vinegar

White wine vinegar

Rice vinegar

ON THE COUNTER

Fresh produce: bananas, potatoes, onions, shallots

TOOLS

Chef's knife

Food processor

Vitamix or high-powered blender

Immersion blender

Meat tenderizer

Instant-read thermometer

Skillets and saucepans of various sizes

Parchment paper

Baking sheet

Loaf pan

Cupcake/muffin tin

Cookie scoop (1 ounce and 1.5 ounce)

Your Nutrition Crash Course

Here's the thing about nutrition: most people overcomplicate it. Yes, you can get down to the nitty-gritty science behind every ingredient you're consuming, including how many calories (sometimes described as macronutrients) it contains, but that's not necessary—and I'll tell you why.

Instead of focusing on research and data, it's much more beneficial, and less stressful, if you just make a point of eating more foods that come from the earth. Once you begin to crowd out the packaged, processed items in your diet with unrefined, nutrient-dense, and colorful foods, I'm confident that you'll start to feel a difference in your body and your energy levels. So many foods and beverages are made with added sugars, artificial ingredients, and unnecessary fillers, so it's up to you to simplify things a bit. And the best way to do that? Cooking for yourself. But don't worry, I'm here to help! The recipes in this book take into account my food philosophies, including the importance of eating a balanced diet that represents all the vital nutritional components your body needs. You don't need to be a dietitian to reap the benefits from this book. But if you want a quick breakdown of the science, I've got you!

The three primary nutrients that your body needs to function, aka the macronutrients, are protein, carbohydrates, and fat. Let's kick things off with protein.

PROTEIN

Protein is major when it comes to exercise and fitness. Not only is it part of every single cell in the human body, protein is also crucial to ensure optimal body performance, such as building and repairing tissues, supporting the immune system, and producing hormones. When you exercise, your muscles actually break down and develop microtears. Protein is responsible for repairing those tiny tears and making the muscles stronger in the process. We like protein!

The second thing you should know is that protein is made up of amino acids. Just as proteins are considered the building blocks of life, amino acids are the building blocks of proteins. But our body can make only some types of amino acids, not all of them, so it's crucial that we get those remaining amino acids, called "essential amino acids," from our diet. To do that, you have two options.

Animal protein: As in, protein that comes from an animal, whether it's meat, dairy, or eggs. These naturally contain all nine essential amino acids.

Plant protein: While most plant foods, such as veggies, grains, and legumes, don't contain complete proteins (with the exception of soy, which you might eat in the form of tofu or tempeh), if you combine a variety of them in your meals over the course of the day, your body naturally completes the proteins by mixing and matching the nine essential amino acids.

Ideal protein consumption varies from person to person depending on activity level, but an easy rule for an adult is about 20 to 30 grams of protein per meal. That would look something like this: 4 ounces of pan-seared wild-caught salmon, 1 cup of sautéed Broccolini, and ½ cup of roasted sweet potato. If you're training hard or lifting heavy weights, it's *normal* for your body to feel hungrier throughout the day. You may want to work in larger portion sizes or increase your snacks during the day, making sure to include quality protein.

CARBOHYDRATES

I think we all know by now that carbs can get a bad rap, but I'd like to set the record straight. Carbohydrates are your body's main fuel source, not to mention that they're responsible for helping regulate stress hormones. And remember how I said that one of my biggest food philosophies is using food as fuel? In my world, carbs are key. It's all about choosing the *right* carbohydrates, as each type affects the body differently.

A simple way to look at carbohydrates is to break them into two categories: simple and complex. Let's consider each type. (You'll see that there are more than two, but bear with me! Keep reading.)

1 **Simple carbohydrates:** Typically grouped with "refined" or sugary carbs, simple carbohydrates are found in foods like white bread, white flour, sugary beverages, pastries, and fruit juices. These foods are digested rather quickly and may cause spikes in blood sugar and insulin, and they don't provide a ton of nutrient value in the form of vitamins, minerals, and fiber. In the short term, simple carbohydrates can leave you feeling crummy and still hungry, which generally leads to a spiral of eating too much sugar and only rarely being satisfied by it. And over time, they can be damaging to the body when eaten in excess, contributing to inflammation from weight gain, chronic fatigue, and an increased risk of disease. Simple carbohydrates are hyper-palatable

and widely available, which makes them hard to avoid. But as you slowly crowd out these foods with more vibrant ingredients, you'll start to have more energy, better gut health (including your digestive system and immune system), less brain fog, and a lower risk of disease.

1.5 **Fresh fruit:** I like to think of whole fruit as somewhere between simple and complex carbohydrates. Fruit digests quickly, much like a simple carb, but fruit is fibrous and rich in minerals and vitamins, moving it closer to a complex carb.

2 **Complex carbohydrates:** Otherwise known as "starchy" carbs, these are the beneficial carbohydrates that your body needs. Because of their complex cellular structure and long molecular chains (no need to get too deep into that here), complex carbohydrates require more work from the body to break down. As a result, they are less likely to cause a rapid spike in blood sugar than simple carbs, and they leave you feeling fuller for longer (which is good!). You can find complex carbohydrates in sweet potatoes, beans, and whole grains— all of which are rich in vitamins and minerals.

I prefer eating more carbs around a killer training session because I know that's when my muscles need fuel the most, especially after heavy lifting. I mostly stick to complex sources of carbohydrates, like organic berries (rich in fiber and perfect for a post-workout smoothie), sweet potatoes (full of vitamin A, vitamin C, and potassium and can be roasted or sautéed as part of lunch or dinner), nuts, seeds, and tons of vegetables. I recommend pairing carbohydrate-rich snacks, such as fruit, with a healthy fat or protein, such as almond butter, to help stabilize your blood sugar and keep you feeling satiated for longer.

Fiber is also a complex carbohydrate found in fruits and vegetables. Unlike fats, proteins, and other carbohydrates, which are broken down and absorbed by the body, fiber isn't actually digested. Instead, it passes *through* your digestive system relatively intact. It not only encourages the elimination of waste (woo-hoo!) but also feeds the beneficial bacteria in your gut. You can think of fiber as a broom, sweeping out all the extra toxins from your body. And it's another one of those "keeps you fuller for longer" foods, so make sure you get enough every day (around 25 to 35 grams total). To do this, try incorporating more fiber-rich chia seeds, flaxseeds, or hempseeds into your smoothies and eating whole fruit (the skin is packed with fiber, remember?), nuts, seeds, and vegetables.

FAT

Fat plays a huge role in helping your body absorb nutrients, build cell membranes, insulate the nervous system, and protect the organs. And it's essential to brain health.

That's right, fats are *good* for your body and should ideally be consumed with every meal. For the same reasons that your body needs essential amino acids to support all of its physiological systems, you need essential fatty acids. There are two types of essential fatty acids—omega-3 and omega-6—but it's the omega-3s that deliver the biggest anti-inflammatory, health-boosting benefits. While omega-6 fatty acids aren't necessarily bad for you, they're commonly found in processed snacks, fast food, fatty meats,

soybeans (including soybean oil), and corn, things that a lot of Americans are over-consuming. Instead, we should be striving to eat more omega-3-rich foods, such as wild-caught salmon and tuna, nuts and seeds (flaxseeds, hempseeds, walnuts, chia seeds), and extra-virgin olive oil to help compensate.

The other fun fact about healthy fats is that they not only decrease your risk of disease, but they also help your body absorb other nutrients. Take fat-soluble vitamins, for example. These include vitamins A, D, E, and K, which all play a major role in your overall wellness. That's why when I eat dark leafy greens, mushrooms, or squash, I always make sure to include a drizzle of extra-virgin olive oil, a few slices of avocado, or a sprinkle of seeds on top. Overall, I love including healthy fats throughout my day because they keep me feeling full and satisfied and can help curb cravings.

MICRONUTRIENTS

Micronutrients are essential for maintaining your health and well-being. That's because this collection of nutrients is essential for maintaining a strong immune system, a healthy cardiovascular and circulatory system—and pretty much every other vital function in your body. The best way to ensure you're getting sufficient micronutrients is to follow my golden rule: the more colors you eat, the more nutrients you get! A well-rounded, colorful diet is full of wholesome foods such as tubers (potatoes, ginger, turmeric), fish, antioxidant-rich oils (extra-virgin olive oil), nuts, seeds, fruits, and a variety of veggies. And trust me when I tell you that the *Good Eats* recipes will hook you up.

Your Starter Guide for Success

So we've talked about my basic philosophy, even had a little science sesh, and now it's time for you to dig in and put all of this to work in real life. But don't worry. Remember when I said this would be easy *and* fun? I meant it! In order to set you up for success—and ensure that you never get overwhelmed—I've put together my top tips for staying consistent and building the kind of life that feels *good*.

Drink more water. Being properly hydrated leads to more energy, better digestion, more satiety after meals, and overall positive body function (not to mention what it can do for your skin—hello, glow!). Aim for 75 to 100 fluid ounces daily. Grab a reusable water bottle, and fill it up multiple times throughout the day (depending on how many ounces it holds). Try adding fresh fruit and/or herbs to elevate the flavor.

Consume a variety of nourishing foods, especially vegetables. Growing up, did anyone ever tell you to fill half your plate with veggies? Yes? I hope so! My goal with this book is to have you really start thinking about the foods you consume and how they'll benefit your body. Even with our busy lifestyles, it's so important to take care of ourselves, and that means realizing the impact food has on our overall health and well-being. So, yes, please remember to fill half your plate with nutrient-dense veggies that nourish your body with every bite.

Make a plan. I find that even if I don't meal-prep, taking a little bit of time on Sundays to map out my meals for the week really sets me up for success. I pick out the recipes I want to make, craft my grocery lift, and hit the store with a game plan. If you think ahead and prepare, you'll end up with healthier options, less food waste, and—my personal favorite—a fully stocked fridge and pantry. I tend to make a little extra food for dinner so we can have leftovers for at least one lunch the following day. Major time-saver!

Eat foods you enjoy (but be open to trying new things). When you're deciding which recipes to cook from this book, start with things that include ingredients you know you love (and that also love your body back, which is a given with these recipes). After that, get out of your comfort zone and try something new. Certain foods take on a whole new personality when they're cooked in different ways—be adventurous!

Be intuitive. Take note of how you *feel* throughout the day. Which foods fuel your day? Which foods leave you feeling crummy? What's your happy place when it comes to hydration? Which meals affect your sleep, for better or for worse? Jot anything down in the Notes app on your phone—small realizations can have lasting impact and help dictate your food choices moving forward.

This book features some of my go-to recipes that I've been making for years, and others that are entirely brand-new. I hope they bring you as much joy as they've brought me—someone who's seen firsthand just how powerful good food (and the company you enjoy it with) can be. So whether you're ready to make healthy changes, or excited to re-create some childhood favorites, I truly hope you enjoy cooking your way through these recipes. Let's do this! Let's do this!

two

BREAKFAST

Anyone else wake up hungry? 'Cause, same. Breakfast is one of those things I look forward to every morning because it's an opportunity for both my body and my taste buds to thrive. However, if you incorporate intermittent fasting into your routine (I know there are a lot of you out there who do), it can be one of the easiest meals to skip. Eating something nutritious, even if it's on the lighter side, first thing in the morning sets the tone for the rest of the day, keeping you fueled from the get-go. And I'm pretty sure that once you try a couple of these recipes, you'll never again think twice about whipping up breakfast.

As for what makes the perfect breakfast, I suggest having something that hits all the macros (carbohydrates, fat, and protein) to keep you feeling full and fueled until lunch (or at least for a few hours, if you're like me). You can expect a variety of my favorite breakfasts, from grab-and-go Twenty-Minute Paleo Granola to sit-down meals like Banana Chai-Spice Waffles with Whipped Honey Butter.

Twenty-Minute Paleo Granola

You'll always find a big batch of this granola in our fridge. I'm a sucker for crunch, so I'll typically throw a handful on top of my smoothies; have a bowl of it with almond milk, fresh berries, and cinnamon (it's *the* best cereal); or grab a handful as a snack more than once throughout the day. Store-bought granola may seem super convenient, but most brands include unnecessary added sugar. That's why I created this easy-to-make, low-sugar alternative, which you can customize by switching up the seeds and nuts you use and incorporating other add-ins. I've included two of my favorite variations here. It's one of my most popular recipes!

Makes 3 to 4 cups

½ cup raw walnuts

⅓ cup raw pecans

⅓ cup raw pumpkin seeds

⅓ cup sliced raw almonds

¼ cup dry-roasted or raw macadamia nuts

3 tablespoons whole flaxseeds

3 tablespoons raw hempseeds

⅓ cup finely shredded unsweetened coconut

¼ cup coconut oil, melted

2 tablespoons maple syrup

1 tablespoon arrowroot starch

1 teaspoon vanilla extract

½ teaspoon ground cinnamon

Pinch of sea salt

For Peanut Butter Granola: Stir ½ cup raw peanuts and 2 tablespoons peanut butter into the mixture before baking.

For Chai-Spice Granola: Stir 1½ teaspoons Chai Spice (page 33) into the mixture before baking.

Preheat the oven to 325°F. Line a baking sheet with parchment paper and set aside.

Place the walnuts, pecans, pumpkin seeds, almonds, macadamias, flaxseeds, and hempseeds in a food processor, and pulse a few times, just enough to chop the mixture slightly. (You could also use a sharp knife to chop them on a cutting board.) Transfer the mixture to a large bowl, add the remaining ingredients, and toss to combine.

Pour the mixture onto the prepared baking sheet, spreading it with a spatula into an even but thick layer. This will create larger pieces of granola. Bake for 12 to 15 minutes, or until golden brown, and let cool for 5 minutes. Without disturbing the granola, immediately transfer the pan to the freezer for 15 minutes to let the coconut oil harden and allow chunks to form.

Break up the chilled granola into chunks, and store it in an airtight container. It keeps in the refrigerator for up to one month.

Note: If you're like me and think the chunks are the best part of granola, the trick is to let the pan of granola harden in the freezer after it comes out of the oven and has cooled. Store it in the fridge both for freshness and to allow the chunks to stay together.

Homemade Cinnamon Applesauce

I grew up on a small farm with animals and all kinds of fruit trees, including quite a few apple and cherry trees. My sister and I used to bag up the cherries and sell them on the side of the road by our house—better than lemonade, no? We also made countless recipes with the apples we grew; this applesauce is one of them. My mom no longer lives on the farm, but let me tell you, the second apple season hits, you know I'll be making more of this cinnamon applesauce. I especially love it on a chilly morning.

Makes 3 cups

8 to 10 medium apples, unpeeled (I like Galas, but any variety will work), cored, and chopped

Juice of 1 lemon

½ teaspoon ground cinnamon

¼ teaspoon ground cloves

Combine all the ingredients in a large pot. Cover and bring the mixture to a boil over medium heat. Stir, and reduce the heat to low. Simmer for 30 minutes, or until the apples are soft. Use a potato masher or fork to mash the apples to your desired consistency. If you prefer a chunky applesauce, don't mash all the way. If you prefer smooth, an immersion blender works great. Serve warm, at room temperature, or chilled.

Store in an airtight container in the fridge for up to one week.

Sweet Potato Toast Three Ways

Toast has a special place in my heart. Not just because I was obsessed with eating cinnamon-and-sugar toast growing up but because I, along with my sister, Maddie, and her best friend, Alissa, own a few Toast Society Cafes in Las Vegas. Our vision was to combine beautiful presentation with wholesome food, and the menu I curated showcases all kinds of nourishing and customizable options that accommodate all dietary needs—superfood smoothies, lattes, chia bowls, and, of course, toast. I'm always playing around with new combinations, but sweet potato toast is my current obsession. After multiple rounds of testing, we found that Japanese sweet potatoes work best in terms of taste and texture.

Serves 3

Preheat the oven to 375°F.

Place the sweet potatoes on a baking sheet and bake for 45 minutes. Let them cool completely, about 40 minutes. (This softens the potato and makes it easier to slice evenly.)

Using a serrated knife, slice the potato into ¼-inch "toasts." Remove the skin from around the outside of each slice.

Turn the broiler on high (500°F). Return the toasts to the baking sheet, and cook them on the center rack of the oven until golden brown, 5 to 7 minutes per side.

Top the toasts with any of the combinations here, or come up with your own.

2 medium Japanese sweet potatoes, unpeeled

House Favorite

1 small avocado, cubed

2 tablespoons crumbled feta

4 cherry tomatoes, halved

1 hard-boiled pasture-raised egg, diced

1½ teaspoons extra-virgin olive oil

¼ teaspoon black sesame seeds

Pinch of sea salt

Pinch of chili flakes

Small handful of microgreens

Perfect Pear

2 tablespoons goat cheese

½ pear, stemmed, seeded, and thinly sliced

2 tablespoons crushed or chopped walnuts

½ tablespoon honey

¼ teaspoon ground cinnamon

Sweet Tooth

2 tablespoons Better-for-You Nutella (recipe follows)

½ banana, sliced

3 strawberries, hulled and sliced

½ tablespoon honey

1 teaspoon raw hempseeds

¼ teaspoon ground cinnamon

Better-for-You Nutella

Realizing how easy it is to make some of your favorite store-bought foods at home is wild, especially when they come out even better than the original. When I nailed this duplicate for the iconic chocolate and hazelnut spread, I knew that I could do *anything*. Slather it over Sweet Potato Toast, use it in baking, or set some out in a bowl on its own and call it a dip.

Makes 1¼ cups

Preheat the oven to 400°F.

Spread the hazelnuts on a baking sheet and bake for 10 minutes. Shake the pan to toss, and bake for 5 more minutes. Let cool for 5 minutes.

Process the roasted hazelnuts in a food processor until they reach a creamy nut-butter consistency, 3 to 5 minutes. Add the remaining ingredients, and process until smooth. Keep in an airtight jar or container in the fridge for up to two weeks.

1½ cups raw hazelnuts, peeled or unpeeled

¼ cup unsweetened nondairy milk (e.g., almond milk, coconut milk)

2 tablespoons maple syrup

2 tablespoons raw cacao powder

1 tablespoon coconut sugar

½ teaspoon vanilla extract

Pinch of sea salt

Banana Chai-Spice Waffles
with Whipped Honey Butter

We all love those cozy weekends when you can catch up on some sleep, stay in your pajamas till noon, and enjoy a leisurely waffle breakfast. That said, no one wants to spend a ton of time making those waffles. So I simplified things *way* down by calling for all the ingredients to be combined in a blender, then pouring the batter straight into a waffle maker (or onto a griddle for pancakes, if preferred). You're welcome! Can we also talk about how this whipped honey butter will change your life? It takes a whopping four minutes to make and keeps fresh for up to one month. My husband, Bridger, and I love these waffles so much that we usually make a double batch and keep the cooked waffles in the fridge. Then, whenever the mood strikes, we just need to pop one in the toaster.

Makes 4 medium waffles

Make the honey butter: In a large microwave-safe bowl, combine the ghee and honey. Heat in the microwave for 15 seconds, until just softened. Add the vanilla and cinnamon, and whisk the mixture for 3 to 4 minutes, until fully combined and fluffy. Store any extra honey butter in a sealed container at room temperature (ghee doesn't contain milk solids, making it stable at room temp) or in the fridge for up to one month.

Make the chai spice: Combine all ingredients in a small jar. Cover with a lid, and shake until well combined. Store in a cool, dry place.

Make the waffles: Preheat a waffle maker.

Put the eggs, oats, banana, almond flour, almond milk, coconut oil, maple syrup, vanilla, baking soda, and 1 teaspoon of the chai spice in a blender. Blend until completely smooth.

Grease the waffle maker with coconut oil cooking spray and pour some batter onto the maker (the amount will be determined by the size of your waffle iron). Cook the waffle until it is golden brown. Repeat with the remaining batter.

Top the waffles with the whipped honey butter and any other toppings you like, such as the ones listed here.

For the Whipped Honey Butter

½ cup ghee

¼ cup honey

½ teaspoon vanilla extract

¼ teaspoon ground cinnamon

For the Chai Spice

1 tablespoon ground ginger

1 tablespoon ground cinnamon

1 teaspoon ground allspice

1 teaspoon ground cardamom

1 teaspoon ground cloves

1 teaspoon ground nutmeg

Pinch of ground black pepper

For the Waffles

2 large pasture-raised eggs

1 cup whole rolled oats or oat flour

1 ripe banana, mashed

¾ cup almond flour

½ cup unsweetened almond milk

1 tablespoon coconut oil, melted

1 tablespoon maple syrup

½ teaspoon vanilla extract

½ teaspoon baking soda

Coconut oil cooking spray

Fresh fruit, sliced almonds, coconut flakes, maple syrup or honey, for serving

Blackberry Pecan
Baked Oatmeal for Two

I can thank baked oatmeal for single-handedly getting me through my dietetic internship in downtown Seattle. It was the number one thing that made waking up at 5:00 a.m. tolerable. I'd get up, preheat the oven, throw a bowl of oats together, and pop it in. And since it took about thirty-five minutes to bake, I'd get my home workout in before breakfast. (I'm even surprising myself as I type this.) That left a few minutes to shower and get dressed before pulling a perfectly baked dish of oatmeal from the oven and digging into it on the way to the train station. That was my ritual on repeat for my entire clinical rotation. While I know the workouts were part of what helped power me through that intense chapter of my life, the oats kept me in a good mood about the whole crack-of-dawn situation—thank you, baked oats!

Pro tip: Double the recipe for a weekend family brunch, or if you want to make your breakfast for the entire week. It reheats like a dream.

Serves 2

1½ tablespoons coconut butter, melted (or coconut oil), plus more for greasing the ramekins

½ cup unsweetened almond milk

1 large pasture-raised egg

1 tablespoon maple syrup

1 teaspoon vanilla extract

1 cup whole rolled oats

¼ cup roughly chopped raw pecans, plus more for serving

2 tablespoons vanilla protein powder (or substitute with 2 additional tablespoons of oats)

½ teaspoon ground cinnamon

½ teaspoon baking powder

Pinch of Kosher salt

1 cup blackberries (or berries of choice), fresh or frozen and thawed

Honey, for serving, optional

Preheat the oven to 350°F. Grease two 8-ounce ramekins with coconut butter and set aside.

In a medium bowl, whisk together the coconut butter, almond milk, egg, maple syrup, and vanilla. Add the oats, pecans, protein powder, cinnamon, baking powder, and salt, and stir until combined. Fold in the blackberries.

Divide the batter between the ramekins and sprinkle with additional pecans, if desired. Bake for 35 minutes or until the oats are cooked through.

Let the oatmeal cool for 10 to 15 minutes. Top with honey, if desired, and serve.

Aussie Protein Brekky Bowl

One thing I love about traveling is that I get so much inspo for meals I want to make when I'm back home. When my then boyfriend (now husband), Bridger, and I were in Australia adventuring through Sydney, Melbourne, and Adelaide, this bowl was my staple breakfast—or "brekky" as they call it there—and they do it oh-so right. I like going protein heavy for my first meal of the day because it tends to be after my workout (our bodies utilize the amino acids that make up protein to build and repair muscle tissue and bone after training), and because protein helps me stay satisfied and full until my next meal. P.S. You'll definitely want your potatoes cooked like this as often as possible.

Serves 2

In a large skillet over medium-high heat, heat 1 tablespoon of the oil. Arrange the sliced potatoes in the skillet in a single layer, and cook for 2 to 3 minutes, until golden underneath. Season with 1 teaspoon of the salt and a few shakes of pepper, flip the potatoes, and continue cooking for another 2 to 3 minutes. Divide between two bowls.

In a medium skillet over medium heat, heat another tablespoon of the oil. Add the cherry tomatoes and the remaining teaspoon of salt, and cook for about 10 minutes or until the tomatoes start to blister. Add the spinach and garlic powder, toss, and cook for 2 more minutes, until the spinach is just wilted. Divide the mixture between the two bowls.

Return the same skillet to medium heat, and heat the remaining tablespoon of oil. Add the chicken sausage and cook, tossing occasionally, for 4 to 6 minutes, until browned. Divide the sausage between the two bowls.

Return the same skillet to medium-low heat, and heat the ghee. Add the eggs, and, using a silicone spatula, stir in a circular motion, cooking slowly until the eggs are about 80% cooked through . . . that's the key! Divide the eggs between the two bowls and serve. Top with sliced avocado.

3 tablespoons avocado oil or extra-virgin olive oil

½ cup thinly sliced (⅛-inch-thick) small unpeeled potatoes, any variety

2 teaspoons sea salt

Freshly ground black pepper, to taste

1 cup cherry tomatoes, halved

4 cups packed fresh baby spinach

½ teaspoon garlic powder

2 precooked organic chicken sausages (about 3 ounces each), sliced into ¼-inch pieces

1 tablespoon ghee or vegan butter

4 large pasture-raised eggs, beaten

½ avocado, sliced

Dippy Tomato Egg Skillet

If there's one brunch recipe that I get excited to make on the weekends, it's this egg skillet. It mentally transports me right to New York. That's probably because every time Bridger and I visit, we're basically on a food tour—as is the case for all my trips—and we eat our way through the city. The last few times we went, it was pretty chilly out, so most of our time was spent hopping in and out of cafés, trying to refuel and warm up. This skillet dish was the perfect meal for doing just that. Get your toasted sourdough ready for dipping or go full paleo and add sliced and seared chicken sausage after it's done. That swap ends up making this recipe a great high-protein dish too.

Serves 2 or 3

In a large skillet over medium-high heat, heat the oil. Add the onion and pepper, and cook for 3 to 5 minutes, until the onions are translucent. Add the garlic, basil, salt, chili powder, and paprika, toss to combine, and cook for 2 minutes. Pour the marinara into the skillet and cook, stirring well to combine the ingredients, for 2 more minutes, until the sauce is hot. Carefully crack the eggs into the sauce, spacing them evenly, and reduce the heat to medium-low. Cook uncovered for 8 to 10 minutes (or cover to speed up the cooking time), until the egg whites are cooked through and the yolk is cooked to your desired degree of doneness. Sprinkle the cheese on top in the last few minutes to let it melt.

Remove the pan from the heat, and shower with fresh cilantro or parsley. Serve with sliced avocado, sourdough bread, and chicken sausage, if desired.

2 tablespoons extra-virgin olive oil

½ large onion, peeled and diced

¾ cup diced red, yellow, or orange bell pepper

1½ teaspoons minced garlic

½ teaspoon fresh or dried basil

½ teaspoon sea salt

¼ teaspoon chili powder

¼ teaspoon paprika

1 (23.5-ounce) jar marinara sauce (choose one with no added sugar)

6 large pasture-raised eggs

¾ cup shredded hard goat cheese (or cheese of your choice)

2 tablespoons chopped fresh cilantro or parsley

Sliced avocado, for serving

Toasted sourdough bread, for serving

Sliced seared organic chicken sausage, optional, for serving

Fluffy Stovetop Oats
with Almond Butter and Chia Jam

You're going to love this cozy oatmeal bowl, which I have on repeat throughout the winter. It's made with my own raspberry chia jam, and you can use any of your favorite nut or seed butters with it. (I'm a sucker for AB&J anything, so I tend to stick to the recipe.) This dish gives me a nice boost of energy for the day with plenty of protein, fiber, and healthy fats.

Serves 1

Make the jam: Place the raspberries, chia seeds, and sweetener, if using, in a jar. Stir, cover, and let thicken in the fridge for at least 30 minutes. Store, covered in the fridge, up to five days. If you don't have time to thaw the berries beforehand, you can heat the frozen raspberries in a small saucepan on the stove, or in a microwave for 30-second intervals, until liquid. Stir in the chia seeds and sweetener, if using, and let sit at room temperature for 30 minutes to thicken.

Make the oatmeal: In a small saucepan over medium-high heat, bring the nondairy milk or water to a boil. Stir in the oats, reduce the heat to medium-low, and stir in the flaxseed and cinnamon. Cook for about 8 minutes, stirring occasionally, until the oats have absorbed the majority of the liquid. Add the egg white and cook, stirring, until it's completely cooked through, about 1 minute. Stir in the almond butter, and remove the pan from the heat.

Serve the oats with plenty of raspberry chia jam, crushed almonds, and another spoonful of almond butter.

For the Raspberry Chia Jam

1 (12-ounce) package frozen raspberries, thawed

1 tablespoon chia seeds

Splash of maple syrup or raw honey, optional

For the Oatmeal

1 cup unsweetened nondairy milk (almond, cashew, coconut) or water

½ cup whole rolled oats

1 tablespoon ground flaxseed

½ teaspoon ground cinnamon

Egg white from 1 large pasture-raised egg

1 tablespoon unsweetened almond butter, plus more for serving

2 tablespoons raw almonds, crushed or roughly chopped

Breakfast Tostadas
with "Refried" Beans

Mexican-inspired food is a quintessential staple of my diet. Basically, if it includes a tortilla, I'm in. Anytime you want a quick breakfast refresh, try out these tostadas and go nuts with the toppings! I like using organic corn or grain-free tortillas like Siete's coconut and cassava flour tortillas.

Serves 2

Make the beans: In a small saucepan over medium-high heat, bring the pinto beans and their liquid to a simmer. Reduce the heat to medium-low, and cook for 7 to 10 minutes. Every few minutes while the beans are cooking, use a potato masher or fork to mash them, twisting as you press down, until the beans are a relatively smooth consistency. Season to taste with salt and pepper, and remove the pan from the heat.

Make the tostadas: In a medium-sized skillet over medium heat, heat the oil. Add the eggs and cook to your liking, seasoning to taste with salt and pepper.

Preheat the broiler to high (500°F).

Using tongs, place the tortillas on the center rack of the oven, and heat for 2 to 3 minutes, just until they begin to turn golden brown and crisp slightly. No need to flip.

Build the tostadas: Spread each crispy tortilla with beans, and top with eggs, avocado, chili flakes, jalapeño, cilantro, salsa, squeezes of lime wedges, and cheese as desired.

For the "Refried" Beans

1 (15-ounce) can pinto beans, undrained

Kosher salt and freshly ground black pepper, to taste

For the Tostadas

1 tablespoon avocado oil or extra-virgin olive oil

2 to 4 large pasture-raised eggs

2 to 4 tortillas

Kosher salt and freshly ground black pepper, to taste

For Serving

Sliced avocado

Red chili flakes

Sliced fresh jalapeño

Chopped fresh cilantro

Hot sauce and/or salsa

Lime wedges

Crumbled feta or cotija cheese

Blueberry Streusel Muffins

Crumbly coffee cake–like streusel topping takes any muffin to the next level. You can enjoy my healthier version for breakfast, or at any time of day: as a quick bite when you're running out the door, a sweet treat to take to family gatherings, or for the kids as an after-school SOS snack.

Makes 12 muffins

Make the muffins: Preheat the oven to 350°F. Spray a muffin tin with cooking spray, or line the wells with paper liners. Set aside.

In a large bowl, whisk together the eggs, banana, almond milk, applesauce, coconut oil, and vanilla. Sprinkle the flour, coconut sugar, flaxseed, cinnamon, and baking powder evenly over the mixture, and gently fold until combined. Fold in the walnuts and blueberries. Using a cookie scoop or large spoon, pour the batter into the prepared muffin tin, filling each well about three-quarters full. Set aside.

Make the streusel topping: In a medium bowl, stir together the flour, coconut sugar, and cinnamon. Add the coconut oil, and mix with a fork till crumbly. Use your fingers to sprinkle the streusel evenly over each well of muffin batter.

Bake the muffins for 40 minutes or until a toothpick inserted in the center of one comes out clean. Let cool for at least 15 minutes before serving.

For the Muffins

Coconut or avocado oil cooking spray

2 large pasture-raised eggs

1 ripe banana, mashed

⅓ cup unsweetened almond milk

⅓ cup unsweetened applesauce

1 tablespoon coconut oil, melted

1 teaspoon vanilla extract

1½ cups store-bought paleo flour blend or all-purpose gluten-free flour (I like Bob's Red Mill)

⅓ cup coconut sugar

2 tablespoons ground flaxseed

1 teaspoon ground cinnamon

1 teaspoon baking powder

¾ cup chopped walnuts

¾ cup fresh blueberries

For the Streusel Topping

3 tablespoons store-bought paleo flour blend or all-purpose gluten-free flour

3 tablespoons coconut sugar

1 teaspoon ground cinnamon

1 tablespoon coconut oil, melted

Make Your Own Paleo Gluten-Free Flour

Makes 3¼ cups

In a large mixing bowl, stir the ingredients together until completely combined. Store in an airtight container for up to six months in a cool, dry place. Use in place of store-bought gluten-free or all-purpose flour in a one-to-one ratio.

1½ cups almond flour

¾ cup arrowroot starch

½ cup coconut flour

½ cup tapioca flour

Folded Greek Omelet

If you love eggs for breakfast but sometimes want to switch it up, this one's for you. Mediterranean food is my jam, so I updated a plain-Jane omelet by adding fresh tomatoes, Kalamata olives, and oregano. But just in case you need one more reason to make this easy, next-level breakfast, consider that eggs contain all nine essential amino acids (making them a complete protein!). Plus, they're rich in choline, which helps support brain activity. Eggs, anyone?

Makes 1 omelet

1 tablespoon extra-virgin olive oil

½ cup halved cherry tomatoes

¼ cup chopped bell peppers

1 big handful baby spinach

6 pitted Kalamata olives, halved

3 large pasture-raised eggs, beaten

2 tablespoons grated cheese (I prefer hard goat cheese or feta)

½ teaspoon fresh or dried oregano

¼ cup fresh basil leaves

In a medium-sized skillet over medium heat, heat the oil. Add the cherry tomatoes and bell peppers, and cook for 2 to 3 minutes, until just starting to soften. Add the spinach and olives, toss, and cook for another 2 to 3 minutes, until the spinach is barely wilted. Pour the beaten eggs over the vegetables and reduce the heat to low. Cook for 4 to 5 minutes, until the surface of the eggs is just beginning to cook through.

Sprinkle the cheese and oregano on top of the eggs and let cook for 1 more minute. Gently fold the omelet in half and remove the pan from the heat. Top with the basil and serve.

three

SMOOTHIES

There's a lot to love about a smoothie, which is why I'm a big smoothie-for-breakfast kind of girl. They're easy on digestion, are the perfect post-workout fuel, and can be a nice, light option if you're not starving in the morning. Plus, there's nothing quicker to throw together. Smoothies also make great snacks, especially on heavy training days, and when built correctly (as in, perfectly balanced, which all my recipes tend to be), they can be used as meal replacements for lunch or dinner. And if that hasn't sold you, consider that many mamas tell me that their kids, including the pickiest eaters, will drink these smoothies without realizing they're getting quite a few servings of fruits and veggies in that "milkshake." From Thin Mint Chip to PB&J, I'm willing to bet there's at least one smoothie here that will make you a believer too.

Salted Caramel Espresso Smoothie

As much as I'd like to gravitate toward warm and comforting breakfasts when the weather is cooler, the truth is, I enjoy smoothies year-round. They're so convenient, especially when I'm (typically) running late between my morning workout and my morning meetings. And the espresso in this recipe almost makes it feel like I'm enjoying a seasonal coffee drink.

Makes 1 smoothie

Place all ingredients in a high-speed blender, and blend until completely smooth. Enjoy right away.

1 cup unsweetened cashew or coconut milk (page 237, refrigerated or shelf-stable)

¾ cup ice

½ frozen banana

1 espresso shot or 4 ounces of coffee

1 to 2 pitted Medjool dates

1 serving vanilla protein powder

1 tablespoon unsweetened almond or cashew butter

1 tablespoon ground flaxseed

Pinch of sea salt

Thin Mint Chip Smoothie

Growing up, my dad taught me the trick of putting Girl Scout cookies in the freezer to make them even more delicious, and I honestly think it made me more of a well-rounded human. It turns out that when you blend up a rich, chocolatey smoothie with a hint of peppermint and a sprinkling of cacao nibs for cookie-crunch texture, it's a pretty spot-on imitation of the real thing (and it just so happens to be packed with nutrients, like magnesium). If you're a mint lover, I know you'll love this smoothie.

Makes 1 smoothie

Place all ingredients in a high-speed blender, and blend until completely smooth. Top with more cacao nibs, and enjoy right away.

1½ cups unsweetened coconut milk or other nondairy milk (refrigerated or shelf-stable)

¾ cup ice

½ frozen banana

1 to 2 handfuls fresh or frozen spinach

1 serving vanilla protein powder

2 tablespoons cacao nibs, plus more for topping

1 tablespoon raw cacao powder

1 tablespoon raw hempseeds

⅛ to ¼ teaspoon peppermint extract, to taste

Bring-You-Back-to-Life Smoothie

You could also accurately call this the anti-inflammatory smoothie because it's full of healing and invigorating ginger, which we love because of its inflammation-easing anti-oxidants. I include turmeric as another immune-system strengthener. Little-known fact: the active compound in this spice, called curcumin, is better absorbed when paired with black pepper, which is why this recipe calls for just a pinch. But don't worry, you won't taste it!

Makes 1 smoothie

Place all ingredients except the bee pollen in a high-speed blender, and blend until completely smooth. Pour into a large glass or jar, and top with the bee pollen, if using.

1 cup unsweetened coconut milk (refrigerated or shelf-stable)

½ cup ice

⅓ cup frozen raspberries

⅓ cup frozen mango chunks

¼ cup unsweetened coconut yogurt (or full-fat or Greek cow's milk yogurt)

1 serving vanilla protein powder

1-inch piece fresh ginger, peeled

¼ teaspoon ground turmeric

Pinch of ground black pepper

Optional topping:
Pinch of bee pollen

Bring-You-Back-to-Life   PB&J

Thin Mint Chip   Salted Caramel Espresso

Dreamy Green Smoothie

Would I even be a dietitian if I didn't include a green smoothie in this section? This is for those days when you're in desperate need of some nourishing greens that can help replenish your body's supply of nutrients. The avocado and frozen banana make the consistency super rich and creamy (while adding a dose of healthy fats and potassium), and the pineapple lends a hint of tropical flavor. You'll love this for breakfast or as an afternoon snack!

Makes 1 smoothie

Place all ingredients except the chia seeds in a high-speed blender, and blend until completely smooth. Top with a sprinkle of chia seeds.

2 handfuls fresh baby spinach or lacinato kale

1½ cups unsweetened almond milk

½ cup ice

½ frozen banana

⅓ cup frozen pineapple chunks

¼ large avocado

1 serving vanilla protein powder

1 tablespoon fresh lemon juice

½ teaspoon matcha powder

¼ teaspoon spirulina powder

¼-inch piece fresh ginger, peeled, optional

Chia seeds, for serving

PB&J Smoothie

I start most mornings with a smoothie right after my workout—they're a great way to replenish, refuel, and stay full for the next few hours. The secret is to add some type of protein to a post-workout smoothie, whether that's quality protein powder, nut butter, or hempseeds (2 tablespoons of which contain 10 grams of plant protein). It's also fun to add superfoods with incredible benefits, like antioxidant-packed spirulina, and vitamin C–rich camu camu. Feel free to change up the add-ins, but pro tip: make sure to start with small quantities and taste as you go so you don't overwhelm the flavor of the smoothie.

Makes 1 smoothie

Place all ingredients in a high-speed blender, and blend until completely smooth.

1 cup unsweetened almond milk

1 cup ice

½ cup frozen strawberries

1 to 2 handfuls fresh or frozen spinach (I prefer frozen)

1 serving vanilla protein powder

1 tablespoon unsweetened peanut butter

1 tablespoon ground flaxseed

1 teaspoon camu camu powder

¼ teaspoon spirulina

four

SALADS & GREENS

Salads are often ordered with "just" in front of them—"I'll just have a salad, please." Sometimes Just Salad seems like its actual name, but there's nothing "just" about salads in my world! You'll see that salads can be some of the most delicious dishes there are, and not just because they're so good for you (although they definitely rank). They provide the perfect opportunity to combine healthy fats, complex carbs, a variety of veggies, and even fruit to make meals and side dishes that are as flavorful and satisfying as they are nutritious. Being a native of Seattle, where gloomy days can far outnumber sunny ones, I've learned to create salads that can suit any mood and all seasons. And I know that I'm on to something, because even my meat-loving hubby regularly asks me to make these recipes. It's pretty common for me to prepare a single dish for our meal in order to keep things simple, while also making sure I'm covering all the bases with greens, proteins, etc.—hello multitasking. This is why you'll see that a lot of these salads have protein added.

Heavy Rotation
Taco Bowls with Mango Pico

This recipe combines two of my favorite things: tacos and eating my meals from a bowl. Food tastes better that way! This is *always* in our lunch and dinner rotation, and for good reason—it's filling, full of vegetables (you see all those colors?), tastes like you're eating tacos (immediate win), and the fresh mango pico is so good that you could eat it on its own. I created the recipe years ago for this tropical salsa, which we ate on our wedding day in Cabo. Now can you see why I'm obsessed with this bowl?

Serves 2

Make the mango pico: In a medium bowl, toss together all the pico ingredients. Taste and adjust seasonings, adding more lime juice or salt if needed. Refrigerate for 30 minutes before serving. Store in an airtight container for up to four days.

Make the taco bowls: In a large skillet over medium heat, heat 1 tablespoon of the oil. Add the ground turkey and cook, stirring, for 5 minutes, until browned. Add 1 teaspoon of the cumin, the chili powder, oregano, garlic powder, ¼ teaspoon of the salt, the pepper, and ¼ cup water, and stir to combine. Reduce the heat to low, cover, and cook for another 5 minutes, until the water has been absorbed and the mixture is uniform. Remove the pan from the heat.

In a medium-sized skillet over medium heat, heat the remaining tablespoon of oil. Add the sliced peppers and onions, plus the remaining ¼ teaspoon cumin and ¼ teaspoon salt, and cook, stirring occasionally, for about 10 minutes. Cover and cook another 5 minutes or so, stirring occasionally, until the vegetables are charred.

Divide the greens between two bowls, and top with the seasoned turkey, charred onions and peppers, beans, tortilla chips, sliced avocado, cilantro, and plenty of mango pico.

For the Mango Pico

1 large semiripe mango (you want a slight crunch to it), peeled and diced

½ large cucumber, peeled, seeded, and diced

½ red bell pepper, stemmed, seeded, and diced

¼ cup finely diced red onion

¼ cup chopped fresh cilantro leaves

Juice of 2 limes, plus more if needed

½ teaspoon sea salt, plus more if needed

½ tablespoon seeded and finely chopped jalapeño, optional

For the Taco Bowls

2 tablespoons avocado oil

1 pound organic ground turkey or other protein of your choice

1¼ teaspoons ground cumin

1 teaspoon chili powder

½ teaspoon each dried oregano, garlic powder, sea salt

¼ teaspoon freshly ground black pepper

1 large red bell pepper, stemmed, seeded, and thinly sliced

½ medium red onion, thinly sliced

6 cups mixed greens

½ cup "Refried" Beans (page 42)

Handful of tortilla chips

½ avocado, sliced

⅓ cup chopped fresh cilantro

Two Easy Ways to Cut a Mango

First, grab a sharp vegetable peeler. Hold the mango in the other hand with a strong grip, making sure your fingers are out of the way. Place the blade of the peeler against the skin of the mango, wiggle the peeler from side to side to break the skin, then remove the peel in long strips. Once the mango is completely peeled, stand it on one end, position a sharp knife slightly off-center at the top of the fruit, and slice downward along one side of the oval-shaped pit. Repeat on the other side. Cut each mango half into cubes or whatever shape you prefer.

The second way calls for keeping the skin on to start. Stand the mango on its end, stem-side up, then take a sharp knife and slice downward from the top, again slightly off-center, along one side of the pit. Repeat on the other side. Hold one of the halves and make crosswise cuts in the form of a grid (squares) without cutting through the skin. Invert the skin so that the cubes stick out. Use a spoon or paring knife to scoop the cubes off the skin. Repeat with the other half.

Avocado Egg Salad

Ever feel like your lunch routine is getting a little too monotonous? Let me introduce you to my famous Avocado Egg Salad. I swap avo for mayo based on my own preference (I not-so-secretly can't stand mayo), plus the avo adds heart-healthy fats, antioxidants, and fiber. I'll spread this on toast or use it as a dip with brown rice crackers. I'm telling you, it hits the spot every single time. It's super filling, and I can never get enough!

Serves 1

In a medium bowl, gently fold together the eggs, avocado, pickle, onion, dill, scallion, mustard, salt, pepper, and chili flakes. Top with sprouts, additional dill, additional chili flakes, and olive oil as desired. Use the salad as a dip with sliced cucumber or crackers, fold it into endive or lettuce wraps, or pile it on top of toast.

2 hard-boiled pasture-raised eggs, peeled and diced

½ large avocado, mashed

1 medium dill pickle, diced

1 tablespoon diced red onion

1 tablespoon chopped fresh dill, plus more for topping

1 tablespoon chopped scallion (white and light green parts)

1 tablespoon spicy brown mustard

¼ teaspoon Kosher salt

¼ teaspoon freshly ground black pepper

¼ teaspoon red chili flakes, plus more for topping

Sprouts of your choice, for topping

Extra-virgin olive oil, for drizzling

Sliced cucumber, crackers, and endive leaves, for serving

Cilantro Caesar Salad
with Grilled Chicken and Crispy Croutons

In addition to finding a combination of ingredients that imparts lots of flavor and texture, the key to achieving a truly great salad is the dressing. And when it comes to a classic Caesar, you have to nail it—which this recipe definitely does, *and* without dairy. I know I've hit the mark by the way Bridger's eyes light up whenever I mention that I'm going to make this salad. It's a staple in the summer for us!

Serves 4

Make the dressing: Place all the dressing ingredients in a food processor, and pulse until creamy. Transfer the dressing to a jar or small bowl, and refrigerate for at least 30 minutes before serving. Any leftover dressing can be kept in an airtight container in the fridge for up to one week.

Make the croutons: Preheat the oven to 375°F. Line a baking sheet with parchment paper and set aside.

In a medium skillet over medium-low heat, heat the olive oil just until warm. Add the garlic and cook for 1 minute.

In a large bowl, toss the cubed sourdough with the heated oil and garlic, salt, and pepper. Spread the seasoned bread cubes on the prepared baking sheet, and bake for 15 minutes, flipping halfway through, until crisped and golden. Set the croutons aside to cool.

Make the salad: Preheat a grill, grill pan, or skillet over medium heat and add oil.

Cover the chicken breasts with parchment paper and beat them with a meat tenderizer (or rolling pin or small skillet, in a pinch) until they're ¼ to ½ inch thick. Season generously with salt and pepper. Grill or sear the chicken breasts until they are browned and have reached an internal temperature of 165°F. Transfer the chicken to a cutting board, and cut into ½-inch-thick slices.

In a large bowl, combine the romaine and 3 heaping tablespoons of the dressing. Toss well. Add the cilantro and toss again to combine. Top the salad with the grilled chicken, croutons, sliced avocado, lemon slices, hempseeds, pumpkin seeds, and some freshly ground black pepper.

For the Caesar Dressing

⅓ cup extra-virgin olive oil

¼ cup tahini

3 tablespoons lemon juice

2 tablespoons capers, drained if packed in brine, or rinsed if packed in salt

2 garlic cloves, peeled and roughly chopped

1½ tablespoons water

1 tablespoon raw hempseeds

½ tablespoon Dijon mustard

¾ teaspoon sea salt

½ teaspoon freshly ground black pepper

For the Croutons

⅓ cup extra-virgin olive oil

2 garlic cloves, peeled and minced

3 cups cubed sourdough bread

¼ teaspoon sea salt and freshly ground black pepper

For the Salad

1 tablespoon avocado oil

2 large boneless, skinless organic chicken breasts

Sea salt and freshly ground black pepper

3 heads romaine hearts, chopped

½ cup fresh cilantro leaves, roughly chopped

1 avocado, sliced

2 to 3 lemon slices, cut ¼ inch thick

2 tablespoons raw hempseeds

2 tablespoons raw or roasted pumpkin seeds

Chopped Antipasto Salad

There are few things better than a big Italian salad and a charcuterie board . . . and this recipe marries them for the ultimate all-occasion salad. It's perfect for dinner parties, weekday lunches, summer BBQs—you name it. Everyone will love how they get a crunch in every bite, and the classic Italian vinaigrette is next-level.

Serves 2 generously

Make the vinaigrette: In a small bowl, whisk together all the dressing ingredients.

Make the salad: Place all the salad ingredients in a large bowl, and toss thoroughly with the dressing. Top with more freshly ground black pepper and serve.

For the Vinaigrette

3 tablespoons extra-virgin olive oil

1 tablespoon white wine vinegar

½ teaspoon dried oregano

½ teaspoon sea salt

Freshly ground black pepper, to taste

For the Salad

1½ heads romaine hearts, finely chopped

1 cup thinly sliced English cucumber

15 to 20 slices salami, cut into strips

⅓ cup thinly sliced red onion

⅓ cup sliced pepperoncini

¾ cup quartered artichoke hearts, well drained

¼ cup halved cherry tomatoes

¾ cup mixed olives, pitted

¼ cup crumbled feta cheese

Freshly ground black pepper, to taste

RGE Cobb

My mom likes to tell my sister and me that all she craved while she was pregnant with each of us was a Cobb salad from Cafe Nordstrom. (She worked at the store for fifteen-plus years.) Let's just say, if the salad looked and tasted anything like the RGE Cobb, I believe her. Of course, I gave it my Rachael's Good Eats twist, but, Mom, I made this one for you!

Serves 3 or 4

Preheat the broiler to high (500°F).

In a medium-sized skillet over medium heat, heat 2 tablespoons of the avocado oil until it is warm but not smoking. Season the chicken breasts generously with salt and pepper, add them to the skillet, and cook for 4 to 5 minutes on each side, or until they have reached an internal temperature of 165°F. (You can cover the pan for the last few minutes to speed up the cooking time if you'd like.) Transfer the chicken to a cutting board to cool.

In a medium bowl, toss the sweet potatoes with the remaining teaspoon of avocado oil, and season generously with salt and pepper. Spread the sweet potatoes on a baking sheet, and broil for 8 to 12 minutes, flipping once toward the end of cooking. The sweet potato cubes should be tender and slightly golden.

While the potatoes are broiling, season the bacon with a few grinds of black pepper, and cook it in a large skillet over medium heat until crisp, about 4 minutes per side. Or feel free to cook the bacon in the oven so you don't have to flip it.

Transfer the bacon to the cutting board and roughly chop it. Roughly chop the cooked chicken.

Place the chopped lettuce in a large serving bowl or on a platter, and arrange the chicken, sweet potatoes, bacon, cucumbers, eggs, cherry tomatoes, and scallions on top.

In a small bowl, whisk together the olive oil, white wine vinegar, lemon juice, and salt and pepper to taste. Set the bowl beside the salad, and let guests spoon the dressing onto their own salads.

2 tablespoons plus 1 teaspoon avocado oil

2 large boneless, skinless organic chicken breasts, halved lengthwise

Sea salt and freshly ground black pepper

1 medium sweet potato, peeled and cubed

5 strips pasture-raised bacon

2 heads romaine hearts, chopped

3 Persian cucumbers, chopped

2 hard-boiled pasture-raised eggs, cut into wedges

1 cup halved cherry tomatoes

4 scallions (white and light green parts), chopped

¼ cup extra-virgin olive oil

2 tablespoons white wine vinegar

Juice of ½ lemon

Thai Crunch Chicken Peanut Salad

If you're a die-hard crunchy salad lover, I created this one specifically for you. With tender shredded chicken (feel free to use leftover rotisserie chicken here), all the colorful veggies (remember: more colors = more vitamins and minerals necessary for immune function and energy production), and a beyond-delicious peanut dressing (featuring my love language, peanut butter), this salad is sure to be a hit with the whole family.

Serves 4

Make the dressing: In a high-speed blender, blend all the dressing ingredients plus 2 tablespoons of water until completely smooth.

Make the salad: Cover the chicken breasts with parchment paper and beat them with a meat tenderizer (or rolling pin or small skillet, in a pinch) until they're ¼ to ½ inch thick.

In a medium-sized skillet over medium heat, heat the oil. Season the chicken with the salt and pepper, and sear in the skillet for 2 to 3 minutes on each side. Cover the skillet and let the chicken steam until it's cooked through, about 5 minutes more. Remove the pan from the heat, transfer the chicken to a cutting board, and shred it, using two forks.

Place the shredded chicken in a large bowl, add the remaining salad ingredients (except the peanuts), and toss well to combine. Pour the dressing over the salad and toss again to coat. Taste, and add more salt if needed. Chill for 30 minutes in the fridge, then serve with crushed peanuts.

For the Dressing

- ⅓ cup creamy unsweetened peanut butter
- ¼ cup coconut aminos
- 2 tablespoons rice vinegar
- 2 tablespoons toasted sesame oil
- 1 tablespoon raw honey
- 1 garlic clove, peeled
- ½ teaspoon sea salt

For the Salad

- 2 large boneless, skinless organic chicken breasts
- 1 to 2 tablespoons avocado oil
- ½ teaspoon sea salt (plus more, to taste)
- ¼ teaspoon freshly ground black pepper
- 2 cups thinly sliced red cabbage
- 2 cups thinly sliced green cabbage
- 1 red bell pepper, stemmed, seeded, and thinly sliced
- 1 yellow bell pepper, stemmed, seeded, and thinly sliced
- 1½ cups snow peas, roughly chopped
- 1 large carrot, peeled and shredded (about 1 cup)
- 1 cup chopped fresh cilantro leaves
- ½ cup chopped scallions (white and light green parts)
- Juice of 1 lime
- ½ cup crushed dry-roasted or raw peanuts, for serving

Tuna Niçoise Salad

If you're new to niçoise (nee-swahz), it's basically the gold standard for salads that are packed with fresh flavor and multiple textures—salty, crunchy, hearty. It was born on the Riviera in Southern France. You could just toss all the yummy components together, but I'm a sucker for serving meals family-style, so I lay out the ingredients in sections. That way, each person can help themselves to a little bit of everything. Feel free to swap out canned tuna for seared or grilled wild-caught tuna or salmon (or your favorite protein), and don't skimp on the capers: they're tiny but mighty and full of glutathione, the master antioxidant. Also, this dressing is super versatile; it'll go great on anything.

Serves 4

Make the dressing: In a food processor or high-speed blender, blend all the dressing ingredients until smooth.

Make the salad: Preheat the oven to 400°F. Line a baking sheet with parchment paper.

Spread the potatoes on the baking sheet, drizzle with the oil, and season with salt and pepper. Bake for 30 minutes, or until the potatoes are tender.

Set a steamer basket in a small saucepan and add an inch or so of water. Set the pan over medium-high heat and bring the water to a simmer. Add the green beans and steam until bright green and just tender, 10 to 12 minutes. Drain the beans.

Arrange the roasted potatoes, green beans, tuna, cucumbers, hard-boiled eggs, olives, avocado, and radishes in their own sections on a serving platter. Scatter the dill over the top, followed by the capers. Serve with the lemon wedges and dressing on the side.

For the Dressing

⅓ cup extra-virgin olive oil

¼ cup chopped scallions (white and light green parts)

Juice of 1 lemon

1 tablespoon red wine vinegar

1 teaspoon sea salt

½ teaspoon freshly ground black pepper

For the Salad

1½ pounds baby Yukon Gold or new potatoes, unpeeled

1 tablespoon avocado oil

Sea salt and freshly ground black pepper, to taste

12 ounces fresh green beans, trimmed

2 (5-ounce) cans tuna packed in olive oil

2 cups sliced Persian or English cucumbers

4 to 6 hard-boiled pasture-raised eggs, and quartered

¾ cup pitted Kalamata olives

1 avocado, sliced

2 radishes, trimmed and thinly sliced

3 tablespoons chopped fresh dill

2 tablespoons salt-packed capers, rinsed

1 lemon, cut into wedges

Cucumber Sesame Salad

This is the perfect light and refreshing side for a hot summer day—when cucumbers happen to be in season—or as a veg-heavy snack in the afternoon. The best part is that you won't break a sweat while making it, because it's so easy to throw together.

Serves 2 to 4

Score the outside of the cucumbers with a fork. This will allow the slices to absorb more liquid. Slice the cucumbers ¼ inch thick and place the slices in a large bowl. Add the remaining ingredients, and toss to combine. Chill for at least 30 minutes before serving.

This salad keeps well in an airtight container in the fridge for up to three days.

6 Persian cucumbers, unpeeled

3 scallions (white and light green parts), thinly sliced

¼ cup thinly sliced shallots

¼ cup rice vinegar

1 tablespoon coconut aminos

1 tablespoon sesame oil

1 tablespoon sesame seeds

1 teaspoon peeled and grated fresh ginger

1 teaspoon red chili flakes

½ teaspoon sea salt

Butter Lettuce Salmon Salad

I love a good salad. I *really* do. I especially like how just a few quality ingredients can make a super-simple combination come to life. In this salad, tahini lends its signature creamy texture to a lusciously rich dressing, while seared salmon and crisp bacon round things out in the flavor and texture department. Not to mention, a little brain-boosting pick-me-up you'll receive from the omega-3s you find in wild-caught salmon.

Serves 2 generously

Make the dressing: In a medium-sized bowl, whisk together all the dressing ingredients until smooth. Set aside.

Make the salad: In a medium-sized skillet over medium heat, cook the bacon until crisp, about 4 minutes each side. Transfer the bacon to a plate lined with paper towels and set aside.

Wipe out the skillet, return it to medium heat, and heat the avocado oil. Season the salmon with the salt, garlic powder, and pepper, and place it in the hot skillet flesh-side down. Sear the salmon for 4 to 5 minutes. Flip it and cook for another 2 to 3 minutes, until the fish flakes easily.

Transfer the salmon to a cutting board, and use two forks to flake it into bite-sized pieces. Roughly chop the cooked and cooled bacon.

In a large bowl, toss together the lettuce and dressing. Top the salad with the flaked salmon, chopped bacon, avocado, and cucumbers. Finish with additional black pepper and chili flakes.

For the Dressing

3 tablespoons extra-virgin olive oil

2 tablespoons tahini

1 tablespoon fresh lemon juice

¾ teaspoon sea salt

¼ teaspoon freshly ground black pepper

¼ teaspoon Dijon mustard

For the Salad

4 slices pasture-raised bacon

1 tablespoon avocado oil

12 ounces wild-caught salmon

½ teaspoon sea salt

¼ teaspoon garlic powder

Freshly ground black pepper

1 large head butter lettuce, leaves washed, well dried, and torn if large

1 avocado, sliced or cubed

1 cup sliced Persian or English cucumbers

Red chili flakes, to taste

White Bean Tuna Salad

I think we can all relate to reaching for foods that may not be the healthiest when we're busy. Been there! But if you want to feel good after lunch (focused, alert, satiated), you should keep a few simple recipes in your arsenal for those days when you barely have time to think straight. This right here is one of them. It's chock-full of protein, so you know it's going to hold you over until dinner, and it's versatile. You have the option to scoop it onto a bed of greens, toast, or, my favorite, brown rice crackers.

Serves 2

In a large bowl, toss together the tuna, beans, olives (if using), sun-dried tomatoes, parsley, red onion, lemon juice, olive oil, salt, and pepper. Add the arugula and toss again to combine. Top with the sliced avocado, a drizzle of olive oil, and chili flakes.

2 (5-ounce) cans tuna packed in water or olive oil, drained

1 (15-ounce) can cannellini or navy beans, drained and rinsed

½ cup pitted, halved Kalamata olives, optional

⅓ cup diced oil-packed sun-dried tomatoes

⅓ cup finely chopped fresh parsley leaves

¼ cup diced red onion

Juice of ½ lemon

1 tablespoon extra-virgin olive oil, plus more for serving

¾ teaspoon sea salt

½ teaspoon freshly ground black pepper

3 cups baby arugula

1 avocado, sliced

Red chili flakes, for serving

Bridger's Favorite Salad

We all have someone in our lives who's not the biggest fan of vegetables—maybe even you—and that's *okay*! Sometimes all it takes is presenting or preparing foods in a new way to make them more appealing. For Bridger, this salad is *it*. He loves the fresh fruit paired with goat cheese and balsamic dressing. Because, obviously. This dish is such a winner, especially in the summer when you can find the freshest, tastiest fruit available.

Serves 4

4 to 5 large handfuls mixed greens

½ cup strawberries, hulled and cut into matchsticks

½ Honeycrisp apple, cored and cut into matchsticks

⅓ cup crumbled goat cheese

½ cup chopped raw pecans

3 tablespoons balsamic vinegar

2 tablespoons extra-virgin olive oil

In a large serving bowl, combine the greens, half the strawberries, half the apples, half the goat cheese, half the pecans, plus the vinegar and olive oil. Toss thoroughly. Top the salad with the remaining strawberries, apple, goat cheese, and pecans and serve.

Greek Honeymoon Salad

I didn't think it was possible to enjoy Greek salads any more than I already did until I had the authentic version in Greece . . . with every single meal. Sure, a little Mediterranean island magic made it taste even better, and the turquoise-water views and endless pitas didn't hurt either. When I got home, I came up with a version that takes me back to my honeymoon anytime I eat it. Every bite is so fresh, with tons of crisp veggies and an herbaceous vinaigrette. It makes an ideal side to any main dish, or a great first course.

Serves 4

Make the dressing: In a small bowl, whisk together all the dressing ingredients.

Make the salad: In a large bowl, gently toss together the tomatoes, cucumbers, pepper, onion, olives, feta, and garlic. Pour the dressing over the salad, and toss again to combine. Serve immediately or refrigerate for up to 30 minutes for a chilled salad.

Just before serving, gently fold in the avocado. Serve immediately.

For the Dressing

3 tablespoons extra-virgin olive oil

Juice of ½ lemon

1 tablespoon red wine vinegar

1 teaspoon dried oregano

Freshly ground black pepper, to taste

For the Salad

3 Roma or vine-on tomatoes, roughly chopped

2 Persian cucumbers, diced

1 large red bell pepper, stemmed, seeded, and diced

½ red onion, chopped

½ cup pitted, halved Greek olives

¼ cup crumbled feta

1 garlic clove, peeled and minced

1 avocado, cubed

five

SOUPS

Nothing hits home like a good soup. Whether it's brothy, hearty, or silky and creamy, soup will forever be nostalgic to me; it's my go-to when I want to feel nourished from within. Plus, I love the fact that you can easily store a batch for later in the week (or for months in the freezer), which is why I always make a big potful when I know things are going to be hectic (and for pretty much every rainy day). And because soups are also made for dipping, you'd better believe there's a Grilled Turkey and Cheese Sandwich in this section too.

Roasted Tomato Basil Soup
with Grilled Turkey and Cheese Sandwich

Nothing screams cozy comfort like a grilled cheese sandwich with tomato soup, am I right? Cooking it from scratch using wholesome ingredients is key—I know I'm not the only one who had Kraft Singles melted between two pieces of Wonder Bread and dipped in Campbell's Tomato Soup growing up. For my dietitian-approved version, I substitute coconut milk for the dairy in the soup, so it's still super creamy, while the roasted tomatoes, onion, and garlic add that deep flavor you know and love—but, like, elevated! As for the sandwich, I use turkey (for some easy protein) and goat cheese, which I find easier to digest than cow's milk dairy—though you're more than welcome to sub any kind of cheese you want, even vegan. You're going to want to make this whenever fall rolls around, or when you find yourself with extra tomatoes from the garden, or when they're in season at the market. **Photograph on page 82**

Serves 4

Make the soup: Preheat the oven to 425°F.

Place the quartered tomatoes and the garlic cloves on a baking sheet. Drizzle with the olive oil and season with salt; toss to coat. Arrange the tomatoes cut-side up, and roast for 45 minutes or until the tomato skins start to char and wilt.

As the tomatoes roast, heat the avocado oil in a large pot over medium heat. Add the onion and cook, stirring occasionally, for 5 to 7 minutes, until softened. Add the oregano and cook, stirring, for another 2 minutes. Add the balsamic vinegar and cook for another 2 minutes. Stir in the stock and coconut milk, cover, and reduce the heat to low. Simmer while the tomatoes finish in the oven, 30 to 45 minutes. Remove the pot from the heat.

Using tongs, transfer the roasted tomatoes to the pot containing the broth mixture. Add the basil, additional salt, black pepper, and garlic powder, and use an immersion blender to blend the mixture until completely smooth. (You can also do this in a countertop blender, working in very small batches.)

For the Soup

- 4 pounds vine-on or Roma tomatoes, quartered
- 4 garlic cloves, peeled
- 3 tablespoons extra-virgin olive oil
- 2 teaspoons sea salt (plus more, to taste)
- 2 tablespoons avocado oil
- 1 medium white onion, diced
- ½ teaspoon dried oregano
- 1 tablespoon balsamic vinegar
- 4 cups vegetable stock or broth
- ¼ cup coconut milk
- 1 cup packed fresh basil leaves, roughly chopped, plus more for serving
- 1 teaspoon freshly ground black pepper, plus more for serving
- ½ teaspoon garlic powder
- Red chili flakes, for serving, optional

For the Sandwich

- Softened ghee or grass-fed butter
- 8 slices sourdough bread or bread of choice
- 2 to 3 cups shredded cheese (I use hard goat cheese)
- 16 thin slices deli turkey (look for organic or one free of nitrates, hormones, and antibiotics)

Set the soup aside, covered, until ready to serve.

Make the sandwiches: Heat a medium-sized skillet over medium heat.

Spread the ghee on a slice of bread, and place the bread in the hot skillet, ghee-side down. Top bread with approximately ½ cup shredded cheese and 4 slices of turkey. Spread ghee on another slice of bread, and place it on top of the turkey, ghee-side up. Press down on the sandwich firmly with a spatula, reduce the heat to medium-low, and cover. Cook for 3 to 4 minutes, until the bottom slice of bread is golden, and flip the sandwich. Cover and cook for another 3 to 4 minutes, until browned on the second side. Transfer the sandwich to a cutting board, and repeat with the remaining sandwich ingredients.

Cut the sandwiches in half if you'd like. Top the soup with additional basil, black pepper, and chili flakes, and serve with the sandwiches for dipping.

Be careful! Steam escapes violently from hot liquids when they're blended in an enclosed container, potentially resulting in the lid being blown off the container—hot soup exploding everywhere—and burned skin. You can avoid this mishap by not filling the blender container more than halfway, and covering the container with a kitchen towel instead of a lid to let steam escape.

Chicken Noodle Bone Broth Soup

There's really nothing better than classic chicken soup on an overcast Seattle afternoon . . . the sort of weather I'm more than accustomed to. By utilizing bone broth, you can truly elevate a staple recipe by upping the nutrient density. Bone broth is a savory liquid made from simmering marrow-rich animal bones (chicken, beef, turkey) for hours, leaving you with a stock extremely high in essential nutrients like protein, calcium, and electrolytes, which your body needs to replenish itself when it's feeling run-down. To save time, I typically use store-bought organic bone broth. A pro tip: add some hot sauce or kimchi sriracha to this soup to blow your mind.

Serves 4 or 5

Cover the chicken breasts with parchment paper and beat them with a meat tenderizer (or rolling pin or small skillet, in a pinch) until they're about ¼ inch thick. Dice the chicken into 1-inch pieces and set aside.

In a large pot over medium-high heat, heat the oil. Add the carrots, celery, and onion, and cook for 5 to 7 minutes, stirring constantly. Add the diced chicken and cook, stirring, for another 5 minutes, or until the chicken is beginning to turn opaque. Stir in the broth, salt, pepper, thyme, and parsley. Bring the mixture to a boil, add the noodles, and cook on high, uncovered, for 13 to 15 minutes, or until the noodles are cooked to your desired firmness. Reduce the heat to low, and simmer for 5 more minutes to combine flavors.

Ladle the soup into bowls, and top with additional black pepper, chopped parsley, and your choice of hot sauce, if desired.

2 large boneless, skinless organic chicken breasts

2 tablespoons avocado oil or extra-virgin olive oil

4 large carrots, peeled and cut into ¼-inch cubes

4 celery stalks, sliced into ¼-inch-thick half-moons

1 medium yellow onion, peeled and diced

8 cups organic chicken bone broth

2½ teaspoons sea salt

½ teaspoon freshly ground black pepper, plus more for serving

½ teaspoon dried thyme

1 teaspoon dried parsley (or 2 teaspoons fresh parsley)

6 ounces brown rice capellini noodles (or your choice of noodles), broken into thirds if long

Chopped fresh parsley, for serving

Hot sauce or probiotic spicy kimchi sriracha, for serving, optional

White Bean Chicken Chili

Bridger and I ate white bean chicken chili for three weeks straight while I was head-down, trying to perfect the recipe to include in this book. Well, it paid off, because I must say, the ratio of beans to spices to chicken is *muy excelente*. (In fact, this might be my favorite soup recipe of all time.) This is a soup that you can embellish with extra heat if you'd like, or fresh cilantro, avocado, and crumbled cheese for an extra burst of fresh flavor.

Serves 4

In a large pot over medium heat, heat the oil. Add the onion and jalapeño and cook for 3 to 4 minutes, until the onion is translucent. Working with 2 chicken breasts at a time, sear the meat in the same pot for 2 minutes per side, until browned but not cooked through. Transfer the seared chicken to a plate, and repeat with the remaining chicken breasts. Add the garlic to the pot and cook, stirring, for 1 minute, just until the garlic is fragrant. Return the seared chicken breasts to the pot, and add the stock, beans, green chilies, pimientos, cumin, chili powder, oregano, salt, paprika, and pepper. Stir, increase the heat to high, and bring to a boil. Cover, reduce the heat to medium-low, and simmer for 6 to 8 minutes, until the chicken is cooked through. Remove the pot from the heat.

Using tongs, transfer the chicken breasts to a cutting board, and shred them using two forks.

Using a potato masher or silicone spatula, lightly mash the beans in the pot, just two or three times. Return the chicken to the pot, and stir in the lime juice.

In a small bowl, whisk together the arrowroot with 1 table-spoon water. Once the starch is dissolved, add the mixture to the pot and stir. Add the cilantro, cover the pot, and continue cooking on medium-low for about 5 minutes to let the flavors come together.

Divide the chili between bowls, and top with more cilantro, avocado, cotija or other cheese, and red chili flakes.

2 tablespoons avocado oil

1 medium onion, peeled and diced

½ tablespoon seeded, minced jalapeño

4 boneless, skinless organic chicken breasts, butterflied

1 tablespoon minced garlic

4 cups organic chicken stock or bone broth

2 (15-ounce) cans cannellini or white navy beans, drained and rinsed

1 (4-ounce) can mild green chilies, undrained

¼ cup jarred sweet pimientos, drained and chopped

2 teaspoons ground cumin

1½ teaspoons chili powder

1 teaspoon dried oregano

1 teaspoon sea salt

½ teaspoon paprika

Freshly ground black pepper, to taste

Juice of 1 lime

1 tablespoon arrowroot starch or tapioca flour

1 cup chopped fresh cilantro leaves, plus more for serving

1 avocado, sliced or cubed

Cotija or other crumbled or shredded cheese, for serving, optional

Red chili flakes, for serving, optional

Hearty Minestrone
with Toasted Garlic Bread

Minestrone is one of those soups that varies all over the world—there's really no set recipe. But it's a given that it will be hearty, packed to the brim with veggies, and sure to warm you right up. I like to think of it as a full meal on its own, which makes it particularly great for easy weekday lunches or dinners.

Serves 6

Make the soup: In a large pot over medium-high heat, heat the oil. Add the celery, carrots, onion, and garlic, and cook, stirring, for 5 minutes. Add the ground turkey and cook, stirring occasionally and breaking up the meat, for 5 minutes, until browned. Add the broth, tomatoes, potatoes, oregano, salt, Italian seasoning, paprika, and pepper, plus 2 cups water. Bring to a simmer. Cover and simmer for 10 to 12 minutes, until the potatoes are tender. Add the uncooked pasta and the green beans, cover, and simmer for another 10 to 12 minutes, or as specified on the pasta package.

Remove the pot from the heat, and stir in the spinach and parsley. Cover and set aside.

Make the garlic bread: Heat the broiler to high (500°F).

In a small bowl, stir together the ghee, garlic powder, and salt. Lay the bread slices on a baking sheet, and brush the ghee mixture on the bread. Broil for 2 to 3 minutes, until toasted and golden.

Divide the soup between bowls, and serve with the toasted garlic bread.

3 tablespoons avocado oil or extra-virgin olive oil

4 celery stalks, diced

3 large carrots, peeled and diced

1 yellow onion, peeled and diced

1 garlic clove, peeled and minced

1 pound organic ground turkey

6 cups vegetable broth

1 (14.5-ounce) can fire-roasted tomatoes

2 small unpeeled yellow potatoes, washed and diced

1 tablespoon fresh or dried oregano

2 teaspoons sea salt

1½ teaspoons Italian seasoning

1 teaspoon paprika

½ teaspoon freshly ground black pepper

1 cup uncooked brown rice pasta shells or fusilli (or, to make it paleo, substitute an extra potato)

½ cup canned green beans, drained

4 cups packed fresh baby spinach

¼ cup chopped fresh parsley leaves

For the Toasted Garlic Bread

3 tablespoons melted ghee

1 teaspoon garlic powder

½ teaspoon sea salt

6 slices sourdough bread (or your choice of bread)

Rich and Creamy Potato and Leek Soup

Potatoes make everything just a little bit better, but especially in soup. This recipe is rich and velvety, but the thing I like most about it is that you can either purée it to be ultra-creamy or leave it nice and chunky. The bacon-and-chive garnish is a must, and I promise you won't miss the heavy cream or dairy!

Serves 4

In a Dutch oven or large, heavy-bottomed pot over medium heat, heat the olive oil and ghee. Add the potatoes, leeks, and carrots, and cook, stirring frequently, until the vegetables are tender, 12 to 14 minutes. Add the garlic and cook, stirring, for 1 more minute. Stir in the broth, almond milk, salt, pepper, parsley, thyme, oregano, and celery salt, and bring to a simmer. Reduce the heat to medium-low and simmer, covered, for 15 minutes.

In a dry skillet over medium heat, cook the bacon until crisp, about 4 minutes per side. Or cook it in the oven to avoid having to flip the slices. Transfer the cooked bacon to a plate lined with paper towels to drain. Once it's cool, chop the bacon into small pieces and set aside.

Remove the soup from the heat. Using an immersion blender, blend the soup to your desired consistency. You can also use a countertop blender for this step; just remember to work in very small batches and leave the blender cap open so steam can escape.

Divide the soup between bowls, and top it with the crispy bacon and fresh chives.

2 tablespoons extra-virgin olive oil

1 tablespoon ghee or vegan butter

4 to 5 medium Yukon Gold potatoes (about 3 pounds), peeled and cubed

4 large leeks (white and light green parts), trimmed, rinsed, and sliced into thin half-moons

2 large carrots, peeled and chopped

3 garlic cloves, peeled and minced

5 cups organic chicken bone broth

½ cup unsweetened almond milk

1 teaspoon sea salt

1 teaspoon freshly ground black pepper

1 teaspoon fresh or dried parsley

1 teaspoon fresh or dried thyme

1 teaspoon fresh or dried oregano

¼ teaspoon celery salt

6 slices pasture-raised bacon

½ cup chopped fresh chives

six

MAINS

It's hard to play favorites with mealtimes, but I *live* to prepare these main dishes. I've been eating some of them for years, going all the way back to when I was in college and experimenting with cooking after discovering my food intolerances. Others are a part of my go-to rotation of meals that I make for my husband and me. And the rest I created especially for this book after years of hearing what my community craves the most.

With gluten-free and mostly dairy-free recipes that range from super-satisfying veg-centric dishes like Zucchini Lasagna and Goat Cheese–Stuffed Mushrooms to meat- and fish-focused dishes like BBQ Meat Loaf Minis and Pistachio-Crusted Fish Tacos, this chapter features preparations that suit most dietary restrictions and every craving. Although I typically cook these dishes for dinner, all of them would make great lunches too. The pro move is to prepare extra for dinner and save the leftovers for the next couple of days' worth of meals.

Goat Cheese–Stuffed Mushrooms

Mushrooms are incredibly versatile. You can chop them up and throw them into scrambled eggs, grill them for savory, smoky goodness, or sauté them with ghee and garlic for a simple side (see Garlicky Mushrooms, page 181). These stuffed mushrooms might be the best of all because they're the perfect little containers for an unbelievable filling—and a super-quick dinner nonetheless. Don't even get me started on the bite-sized pieces of bacon!

Serves 4

Preheat the oven to 350°F. Line a baking sheet with parchment paper and set aside.

In a medium-sized skillet over medium-high heat, heat the oil. Add the onion and Anaheim pepper and cook, stirring, for 2 minutes. Add the garlic and cook for another minute. Add the turkey, zucchini, fennel seed, basil, salt, and pepper, and cook, stirring frequently and breaking up the meat, for 5 to 7 minutes, until the turkey is browned. Remove the pan from the heat and set aside.

In a small skillet over medium heat, cook the bacon until crisp, about 4 minutes per side. Or bake it in the oven to avoid flipping the slices. Transfer the bacon to a plate lined with paper towels to drain and cool. Chop the bacon into small pieces.

In a large bowl, combine the turkey mixture, chopped bacon, spinach, and goat cheese, and mix with a spatula until the goat cheese is melted and evenly distributed.

Place the mushroom caps on the prepared baking sheet, and divide the filling evenly among the caps, mounding it on top of each. Drizzle each mushroom cap with olive oil, and bake for 15 minutes or until the edges of the mushroom caps have browned and appear slightly roasted.

Top the stuffed mushrooms with additional black pepper and fresh chives or scallions and serve.

1 tablespoon avocado oil

⅓ cup diced red onion

1 Anaheim pepper, stemmed, seeded, and diced

1 teaspoon minced garlic

1 pound organic ground turkey

½ cup finely diced zucchini

½ teaspoon fennel seed

½ teaspoon fresh or dried basil

½ teaspoon sea salt

¼ teaspoon freshly ground black pepper, plus more for serving

3 slices pasture-raised bacon

2 cups lightly packed fresh spinach, finely chopped

½ cup soft goat cheese

4 portobello mushrooms, stemmed, washed, and thoroughly dried

Extra-virgin olive oil, for drizzling

¼ cup chopped fresh chives or minced scallions

Sheet-Pan Sesame Salmon Rice Bowls

As if making your entire dinner on a single sheet pan in under fifteen minutes weren't exciting enough, the Asian-inspired marinade in this bowl is truly out of this world.

Serves 2

Place an oven rack in the center of the oven. Preheat the broiler to high heat (500°F). Line a baking sheet with foil and set aside.

In a deep medium-sized bowl, whisk together the coconut aminos, sesame oil, 1 tablespoon of the avocado oil, ½ tablespoon of the sesame seeds, and ¼ teaspoon salt. Using tongs, place the salmon in the marinade, and gently turn it a few times to coat. Let the salmon marinate for 10 minutes.

In another medium-sized bowl, toss the bok choy halves and sliced sweet potatoes with the remaining tablespoon of avocado oil, plus salt and pepper to taste.

Place the coated salmon filets on the prepared baking sheet, skin-side down, and pour any remaining marinade over the filets. Surround the salmon with the vegetables arranged in an even layer; lay the bok choy cut-side up and the sweet potatoes flat.

Broil until the bok choy starts to char on the edges, 10 to 12 minutes. If needed, you can flip the sweet potatoes once they begin to turn golden. Let the salmon bake for about 8 minutes if you like it rare, or 10 to 12 minutes for fully cooked. If you notice that the salmon is done before the veggies, remove the salmon from the pan and transfer it to a serving plate while the vegetables finish cooking, about 3 more minutes.

Assemble the bowls: Divide the cooked rice between two bowls. Top with the greens, sliced peppers, sliced avocado, warm salmon, and roasted bok choy and sweet potatoes. Sprinkle the scallions and cilantro on top, and drizzle with a bit of olive oil.

For the Sheet-Pan Salmon and Veggies

- 2 tablespoons coconut aminos
- 2 tablespoons toasted sesame oil
- 2 tablespoons avocado oil
- 1 tablespoon sesame seeds
- ½ teaspoon Himalayan pink salt or sea salt, plus more to taste
- 2 (6-ounce) thick wild-caught salmon filets
- 2 baby bok choy, trimmed and halved lengthwise
- ½ medium sweet potato, unpeeled, sliced into ¼-inch-thick half-moons
- Freshly ground black pepper, to taste

For the Bowls

- 1 cup cooked sprouted brown rice
- 2 cups packed mixed greens
- 6 mini sweet peppers or 1 medium yellow or red bell pepper, stemmed, seeded, and thinly sliced
- 1 small avocado, sliced
- ¼ cup slivered or chopped scallions (white and light green parts)
- ¼ cup chopped fresh cilantro leaves
- Extra-virgin olive oil, for drizzling

Better-Than-Takeout Orange Chicken

It took me years to get Bridger off Panda Express in college (sorry / not sorry, babe). The fact that he goes nuts for this recipe is the true test. We love pairing this chicken with brown rice or a big salad. Who knows, your picky significant other might even be duped if you were to throw this meal in its own little takeout box!

Serves 2 to 4

Preheat the oven to 400°F. Line a baking sheet with parchment paper and set aside.

Place the flour, ½ teaspoon of the salt, and the pepper in a large ziplock plastic bag. Shake to combine. Add the cubed chicken, and toss to coat. Spread the coated chicken pieces in an even layer on the prepared baking sheet, and bake for 10 minutes. Flip the chicken pieces and return to the oven for another 5 minutes, or until the chicken is light golden brown.

In a medium-sized skillet over medium-high heat, combine the orange juice, coconut aminos, sesame oil, rice vinegar, ginger, and garlic. Bring to a boil, and reduce the heat to low. Simmer for 10 minutes, stirring occasionally.

Place the arrowroot starch in a small bowl. Add a few spoonfuls of the hot orange juice mixture, and whisk until the starch is dissolved. Return the starch mixture to the skillet and add ¼ cup water. Cook the orange sauce over low heat, whisking constantly, for about 2 minutes, until thickened. Add the honey and the remaining teaspoon of salt, and whisk to combine.

Fold the chicken into the sauce, and cook for 2 to 4 more minutes, stirring occasionally, until the chicken is well coated and warmed through.

Garnish with the scallions and sesame seeds, and serve.

⅓ cup almond or coconut flour

1½ teaspoons sea salt

½ teaspoon freshly ground black pepper

2 boneless, skinless organic chicken breasts, cut into 1-inch cubes

½ cup fresh-squeezed orange juice

⅓ cup coconut aminos

1 tablespoon sesame oil

1 tablespoon rice vinegar

1 teaspoon peeled and grated fresh ginger

1 tablespoon minced garlic

1 tablespoon arrowroot starch

2 tablespoons honey

Chopped scallions, for serving

Sesame seeds, for serving

Honey-Glazed Garlic Chicken Wings

Get these prepped and ready for your next game day. Bridger's a big wing guy, so when I first made these for him and they were gone in 0.2 seconds, I knew it was a 10/10 recipe. The wings come out of the oven super tender, and the sauce has the perfect touch of sweetness from the honey without being too heavy. They're finger-lickin' good, good *for* you, and, TBH, it's hard to make them any other way!

Serves 2 to 4

Make the wings: Preheat the oven to 400°F. Line a baking sheet with parchment paper or aluminum foil, and set a wire rack on top. Spray the rack with the oil and set aside.

Using paper towels, pat the chicken wings completely dry. In a large bowl, whisk together the paleo flour, garlic powder, salt, and pepper. Add the chicken wings and drumsticks, and toss well to coat.

Using tongs, transfer the chicken wings one at a time to the rack, spacing evenly. Spray the wings with more oil spray, and bake for 25 minutes. Turn the wings and return them to the oven for another 25 to 30 minutes, until crisp and cooked through.

While the wings are in the oven, make the sauce: In a small skillet over medium-high heat, heat the oil. Add the garlic and ginger and cook for 1 minute, just until fragrant. Add the coconut aminos, honey, rice vinegar, salt, pepper, and chili flakes, if using, and cook, stirring constantly, for another 1 to 2 minutes. Reduce the heat to low.

Place the arrowroot starch in a small bowl, add a spoonful of the sauce, and stir until the starch is completely dissolved. Add the starch mixture back to the sauce and cook, stirring, until the sauce is shiny and thickened.

Transfer the hot wings to a large mixing bowl and add the sauce. Toss well to coat, and serve immediately.

For the Wings

Avocado oil spray or extra-virgin olive oil spray

20 pasture-raised chicken wings (and/or drumsticks)

⅓ cup paleo baking flour

1 teaspoon garlic powder

½ teaspoon sea salt

½ teaspoon freshly ground black pepper

For the Sauce

1 tablespoon avocado oil

4 garlic cloves, peeled and minced

1 teaspoon peeled and grated fresh ginger

¼ cup coconut aminos

2 tablespoons honey

1 tablespoon rice vinegar

½ teaspoon sea salt

Freshly ground black pepper, to taste

Red chili flakes, to taste, optional

1 teaspoon arrowroot starch

One-Pan Chicken Enchilada Skillet

We love a good deconstructed dish that has the same flavor as the original but cooks in half the time, right? I can't tell you how often I've resorted to this beyond-easy rendition of enchiladas whenever I don't feel like spending a lot of time in the kitchen or I've exhausted all my brain power and want to get us fed on autopilot. Even Bridger, who'd rather eat than cook, loves making this enchilada skillet because it's simple. You prepare it and serve it in just *one pan*. It's customizable too: you can assemble it with whatever veggies you have in the fridge. No trips to the grocery for missing ingredients!

Serves 4

In a large skillet over medium heat, heat the oil. Add the onions and garlic and cook, stirring, for 3 minutes. Add the turkey and cook for 5 minutes, stirring and breaking up the meat, until the turkey is browned. Stir in the zucchini, bell pepper, half the enchilada sauce, the cumin, chili powder, paprika, and salt and pepper. Cook for several minutes, stirring occasionally, until the peppers have softened slightly.

Stir in the remaining enchilada sauce, plus ¼ cup of the cilantro and ¼ cup of the shredded cheese. Add the tortilla strips, stir, and reduce the heat to medium-low. Cover and cook for 10 minutes. Add the remaining cilantro and cheese, and the scallions. Cover and cook for 1 more minute, just until the cheese is melted.

Top with the sliced avocado and red chili flakes and serve.

2 tablespoons avocado oil

½ cup diced red onion

1 teaspoon minced garlic

1 pound organic ground chicken or turkey

2 cups chopped zucchini

1 large red bell pepper, stemmed, seeded, and diced

1 (15-ounce) jar enchilada sauce (I like Siete)

¼ teaspoon ground cumin

¼ teaspoon chili powder

¼ teaspoon paprika

Sea salt and freshly ground black pepper, to taste

½ cup chopped fresh cilantro leaves

½ cup shredded hard goat cheese (or sub your favorite cow's milk or vegan cheese)

4 (6-inch) tortillas, cut into strips (I like Siete)

¼ cup chopped scallions

1 avocado, sliced

1 teaspoon red chili flakes

Crispy Chicken Parm

I went many years without eating chicken Parmesan because I thought it was impossible to prepare without using standard-issue Italian bread crumbs and cow's milk cheese. But then I discovered that you can use *crackers* to create the perfect crispy golden crust, and you can include hard goat cheese for creaminess. The result is a dish that tastes just like the old-school original.

Serves 4

Preheat the oven to 400°F.

    Place ¼ cup of the grated goat cheese, the crackers, flaxseed, oregano, and salt in a food processor, and pulse until the mixture reaches an extra-fine texture. Transfer the crumb mixture to a wide, shallow bowl or small baking dish and set aside.

    Put the beaten egg in another wide, shallow bowl or small baking dish. Prepare an assembly line of shallow bowls containing the chicken breasts, the egg wash, and the seasoned cracker crumbs. Place a large clean plate at the end.

    Using a fork, dip a chicken breast in the egg wash and then in the crumbs, pressing the meat into the breading mixture and repeating on the other side until fully covered. Transfer the breaded chicken to the clean plate, and repeat with the remaining chicken breasts.

    In a large, deep frying pan over medium-high heat, heat the oil. Pan-fry the breaded chicken pieces two or three at a time, 3 to 4 minutes per side, until the breading is a rich golden brown. Transfer the seared chicken to a 14 × 10-inch baking dish, and repeat with the remaining chicken.

    Top the chicken breasts with the marinara sauce and the remaining grated goat cheese. Bake the chicken for 10 minutes, then broil for an additional 2 minutes to brown the cheese. Sprinkle the parsley on top and serve hot.

2½ cups grated hard goat cheese (or your choice of cheese)

1½ cups almond flour crackers or seeded crackers (I like Simple Mills Sea Salt crackers; feel free to substitute about 1 cup almond flour or gluten-free bread crumbs, if you'd prefer)

2 tablespoons ground flaxseed

1 teaspoon dried oregano

½ teaspoon Kosher salt

1 large pasture-raised egg, lightly beaten

2 large organic chicken breasts, butterflied and halved

¼ cup avocado oil or extra-virgin olive oil

1 to 2 cups marinara sauce (such as Primal Kitchen or Rao's)

¼ cup chopped fresh parsley leaves

Teriyaki Meatballs

Meatballs are the ultimate potluck offering or game-day appetizer, but they also make the best meal with rice and veggies. When it comes to leftovers, these meatballs are probably what our household enjoys most because they're super juicy and tender, and they reheat well. I doubled the recipe for you because I know that once you taste them, you'll wish you had twice as many.

Serves 4

Make the meatballs: Preheat the oven to 400°F. Line a baking sheet with parchment paper and set aside.

In a large bowl, combine the ground chicken, almond flour, eggs, scallions, coconut aminos, red onion, rice vinegar, balsamic vinegar, sesame oil, ginger, and garlic powder. Season generously with salt and pepper, combining them thoroughly into the mixture.

With clean, wet hands, roll the meat mixture into 1½-inch balls, and arrange the meatballs on the baking sheet evenly spaced. The mixture should make about 20 meatballs. Be gentle when rolling, and wet your hands as needed to prevent sticking. Bake for 20 minutes, or until an instant-read thermometer inserted into the center of a meatball reads 140°F.

Make the sauce: In a small bowl, whisk the arrowroot starch with 2 tablespoons of warm water until the starch dissolves and is smooth. Set aside.

In a large skillet over medium heat, stir together the teriyaki sauce and pineapple juice. Add the arrowroot mixture and stir to combine. Bring the sauce to a simmer, reduce the heat to low, and cook for 10 minutes or until it looks silky.

Add the hot meatballs to the sauce, and toss gently to coat. Top with the sliced scallions and sesame seeds and serve.

For the Meatballs

- 2 pounds organic ground chicken (or substitute ground turkey or beef)
- 1½ cups almond flour
- 2 large pasture-raised eggs, lightly beaten
- ⅓ cup chopped scallions (white and light green parts)
- ¼ cup coconut aminos
- ¼ cup finely diced red onion
- 1 tablespoon rice vinegar
- 1 tablespoon balsamic vinegar
- 1 tablespoon toasted sesame oil
- 1 teaspoon ground ginger
- ¼ teaspoon garlic powder
- Kosher salt and freshly ground black pepper

For the Sauce

- 1 tablespoon arrowroot starch
- 1 cup teriyaki sauce (I like Primal Kitchen's No Soy Teriyaki Sauce and Marinade)
- ½ cup unsweetened pineapple juice
- 3 scallions (white and light green parts), sliced
- 1 tablespoon sesame seeds

Salmon Skewer Gyro Bowls
with Tzatziki

In high school, when Bridger and I first started dating, I spent my summers working for a Greek restaurant that set up at fairs and weekend markets. One year, I somehow convinced Bridge to work with me, and we ended up eating endless gyros and Greek fries with tzatziki. This dish is my grown-up revamp with salmon skewers (though chicken is amazing here too), veggies, rice, and homemade tzatziki. You could say it was love at first bite.

Serves 2 to 4

Make the tzatziki: In a medium bowl, whisk together all the tzatziki ingredients until well combined. Cover and chill while you prepare the bowls.

Make the bowls: Bring 1¼ cups water to a boil in a medium saucepan. Add the rice, cover, reduce the heat to medium-low, and cook until the water is absorbed, 10 to 15 minutes. Remove the pan from the heat, fluff the rice, and replace the lid. Set aside.

In a medium-sized bowl, gently combine the salmon with 1 tablespoon of the oil, the oregano, salt, and pepper. Let the salmon marinate at room temperature for 10 minutes.

On 8-inch-long skewers, alternate pieces of the salmon with rolled-up or ribboned zucchini and squash slices. Season the assembled skewers with additional oregano, salt, and pepper as desired.

In a large skillet over medium-high heat, heat the remaining 2 tablespoons of oil. Add the skewers, working in batches if needed, and sear for about 2 minutes per side. Squeeze juice from the lemon halves over the skewers, cover the pan, and reduce the heat to medium-low. Let the skewers steam for about 5 minutes, until the salmon is tender and flaky. Repeat with the remaining skewers. Transfer the cooked skewers to a board or plate.

Divide the rice between bowls, and top with the Greek salad, salmon skewers, and tzatziki.

For the Tzatziki

1 cup plain Greek yogurt (or nondairy Greek yogurt)

½ large cucumber, grated (any variety)

1½ tablespoons minced fresh dill

Juice of ½ lemon

1 garlic clove, peeled and minced

1 teaspoon sea salt

¼ teaspoon garlic powder

For the Bowls

1 cup uncooked white jasmine rice, rinsed well

1 pound wild-caught salmon filets, cut into 1-inch cubes

3 tablespoons avocado oil or extra-virgin olive oil

1 tablespoon dried oregano, plus more as needed

½ teaspoon sea salt, plus more as needed

¼ teaspoon freshly ground black pepper

1 small green zucchini, sliced very thinly lengthwise (a mandoline or vegetable peeler works great here)

1 small yellow squash, sliced very thinly lengthwise (a mandoline or vegetable peeler works great here)

1 lemon, halved

2 cups Greek Honeymoon Salad (page 81)

Baked Crusted Halibut

Halibut is a lean white fish with mild flavor and a thick, flaky texture. This preparation makes a juicy, melt-in-your-mouth dish, baked with the most delicious crumbly lemon crust on top. It's a fan favorite in my family, and I think it'll blow your mind too. I recommend pairing it with Garlicky Mushrooms (page 181) and Broccolini with Caramelized Shallots (page 182).

Serves 2

Place a rack in the center of the oven. Preheat the oven to 400°F. Line a baking dish with parchment paper and set aside.

In a small bowl, whisk together the coconut flour, coconut oil, lemon juice and zest, garlic powder, chili flakes, white pepper, and ½ teaspoon of the salt. Set aside.

Pat the halibut dry, season with the remaining ½ teaspoon salt, and spray with the cooking spray. Lay the fish skin-side down in the prepared baking dish. Spoon the coconut flour mixture on top of each filet, gently pressing down to help it stick and form a crust. Spray the tops again with cooking spray.

Bake on the center rack for 12 to 15 minutes, until the fish is just opaque and flakes with a fork. The crust will turn golden—but keep an eye on it so it doesn't burn. If it starts to get too dark before the fish is done, cover the dish with foil.

Serve hot with your favorite sides.

3 tablespoons coconut flour

2 tablespoons coconut oil, melted

Juice and zest of ½ lemon

½ teaspoon garlic powder

¼ teaspoon red chili flakes

¼ teaspoon ground white pepper

1 teaspoon sea salt

2 (8-ounce) wild-caught halibut filets

Avocado or olive oil cooking spray

Juicy Turkey Burgers
with Caramelized Onions

Our weeknight dinner rotation isn't complete without some variation of these turkey burgers. It's been that way for me since I was little, with my mom using all kinds of fresh ingredients to spice them up. I love that these burgers are lean and easy to sneak extra veggies into, especially spinach, which has high amounts of vitamin C. Topping the burgers with caramelized onions takes them to a whole new level, and unlike standard-issue beef burgers, they hold over well—I'll eat one cold the next day for lunch when I'm super busy. Once you make these burgers, I'm sure you'll keep them in your rotation too. You can enjoy this burger on a bun, in a lettuce wrap, or straight-up on top of your salad.

Makes 4 burgers

Make the caramelized onions: In a large skillet over medium-high heat, heat the avocado oil. Add the onion, salt, and pepper, and cook, tossing frequently, for 10 to 15 minutes, until the onions are golden brown and caramelized. Remove the pan from the heat and set aside.

Make the burgers: Place the turkey, bell pepper, spinach, red onion, feta, sun-dried tomatoes, garlic, fennel seed, basil, salt, and pepper in a large bowl. Mix thoroughly with your hands or a silicone spatula. Wet your hands, and form the mixture into four patties. (It will be a bit sticky; that's normal.)

In a large skillet over medium heat, heat the oil. Add the patties, and brown for 3 to 4 minutes per side. Add the broth, cover the pan, and reduce the heat to medium-low. Steam the patties for 5 to 7 minutes, until the internal temperature reaches 165°F.

Serve the burgers on buns or in lettuce wraps, and top with the caramelized onions, avocado, and tomato.

For the Caramelized Onions

1 tablespoon avocado oil

1 medium white onion, peeled and thinly sliced

½ teaspoon sea salt

¼ teaspoon freshly ground black pepper

For the Burgers

1 pound organic ground turkey

½ large bell pepper, stemmed, seeded, and diced

½ cup packed fresh spinach, finely chopped

⅓ cup diced red onion

¼ cup crumbled feta

¼ cup sun-dried tomatoes, drained and chopped

1 teaspoon minced garlic

1 teaspoon fennel seeds

1 teaspoon dried basil

½ teaspoon sea salt

Freshly ground black pepper

1 tablespoon avocado oil

3 tablespoons organic chicken broth or water

For Serving

Gluten-free buns or large lettuce leaves for wraps

Sliced avocado

Sliced tomato

Whole-Roasted Lemon and Rosemary Chicken

Roasted chicken is one of those versatile dishes that is delicious in its own right but can be repurposed a million different ways: add the shredded leftover meat to salads, tacos, soups, nachos—you name it. This version is extra flavorful thanks to fresh rosemary (I grab some sprigs from our garden), lemons, and onion. It's also pretty low fuss once you throw it in the oven—all that's left to do is pull together your favorite sides.

Serves 4 to 6

2 tablespoons avocado oil

6 sprigs fresh rosemary

⅓ cup ghee or vegan butter, melted

1 tablespoon minced garlic

1 teaspoon dried thyme

1 teaspoon sea salt

½ teaspoon freshly ground black pepper

½ teaspoon paprika

1 (3-to-5-pound) pasture-raised whole chicken, neck and giblets removed, if included

1 large white onion, peeled and quartered

2 lemons, quartered

½ cup organic bone broth or chicken broth

Preheat the oven to 400°F. Oil a large Dutch oven or a 13 × 9-inch baking dish with the avocado oil and set aside.

Chop the leaves from 4 of the rosemary sprigs. In a medium-sized bowl, stir together the ghee, chopped rosemary, garlic, thyme, salt, pepper, and paprika. Set aside.

Dry the chicken thoroughly with paper towels, and set it in the prepared Dutch oven or baking dish. Stuff the cavity with the onions, lemons, and the 2 remaining rosemary sprigs. Any pieces of onion or lemon that can't fit inside can sit next to the chicken in the dish. Brush the seasoned ghee all over the chicken. Add the broth to the base of the dish, and roast the chicken, uncovered, for 30 minutes.

Carefully brush the chicken with the roasting juices from the bottom of the pan. Return the chicken to the oven and continue to roast, uncovered, for another 40 minutes, or until the internal temperature reaches 165°F when measured at the thickest part of the thigh. Depending on the size of your chicken, you may need to continue roasting in 10-minute increments. If the skin begins to get too dark, cover with a lid or foil.

Let the chicken cool slightly before carving and serving. To carve, place the chicken breast-side up on a cutting board. Pull one leg and thigh out away from the body of the chicken, and use a large chef's knife or carving knife to cut through the connective joint, removing the entire leg and thigh. Separate the drumstick from the thigh by forcefully pushing the knife

straight down at the joint and cutting through. Repeat with the other leg. Next, make a cut along one side of the breast-bone from the neck cavity to the tail end, pulling the breast meat away from the bone as you cut. Repeat with the remaining breast, then place each breast skin-side up on the cutting board and remove the wing portion. From there, cut the breast meat into smaller pieces and serve.

One-Pan Chicken Sausage Bake

Rachael's Good Eats fans request easy one-pan meals over and over. Well here you go: *the* most delicious sausage bake with roasted veggies and potatoes. I don't think I'll ever get tired of this meal. The flavor is beyond, especially with the fresh herby kick at the end. Don't have one of the veggies listed? Easy! Swap with another of your favorites.

Serves 2 to 4

Preheat the oven to 400°F. Line two sheet pans with parchment paper (or leave bare and spray with oil), and set aside.

In a large bowl, toss together the chicken sausage, potatoes, carrots, parsnips, bell pepper, avocado oil, nutritional yeast, oregano, onion powder, garlic powder, thyme, salt, and pepper.

Divide the mixture between the two prepared baking sheets in a single, even layer, making sure not to crowd the pan. Bake for 30 minutes, flip and toss the ingredients, and continue baking for another 15 minutes, or until the meat and veggies are golden and slightly charred in spots.

Sprinkle the fresh parsley over everything and serve immediately. This is great on its own or served on a bed of greens, topped with avocado and a drizzle of olive oil.

4 organic chicken sausages, any variety, precooked and sliced into ½-inch-thick rounds

10 fingerling potatoes, unpeeled, cut in half

2 large carrots, peeled and cut into ¼-inch-thick coins

1 large parsnip, peeled and cut into ¼-inch-thick coins

1 medium bell pepper, stemmed, seeded, and roughly chopped

2 tablespoons avocado oil

1½ tablespoons nutritional yeast

1 tablespoon dried oregano

2 teaspoons onion powder

2 teaspoons garlic powder

1 teaspoon dried thyme

1 teaspoon sea salt

Freshly ground black pepper, to taste

¼ cup chopped fresh parsley leaves, for serving

Spinach or mixed greens, optional, for serving

Sliced avocado, optional, for serving

Extra-virgin olive oil, optional, for serving

BBQ Meat Loaf Minis

Growing up, I had meat loaf more times than I can remember, and I loved it every. Single. Time. Even though it seems impossible to improve on the memory of my dad's original version, Wonder Bread crumbs and all, this new and improved BBQ meat loaf 2.0 is to die for. I'm also very into the fact that the mini loaves make it easy to store leftovers and reheat them for lunches during the week.

Makes 8 to 12 mini meat loaves

Preheat the oven to 400°F. Drizzle or spray the bottom of each cavity of an 8-cavity mini loaf tin or a standard muffin tin with olive oil and set aside.

Place the crackers in a ziplock plastic bag, and crush them with the bottom of a glass to create a fine powder. Transfer the cracker crumbs to a large bowl. Add the ground beef, ground turkey, onion, bell pepper, feta, scallions, ¼ cup of the barbecue sauce, egg, coconut aminos, jalapeño (if using), garlic, salt, pepper, and smoked paprika. Mix gently to combine.

Divide the meat mixture into the cavities of the prepared loaf pan or muffin tin, and smooth the top of each mini loaf with a silicone spatula. Bake for 20 minutes. Carefully remove the pan from the oven and spread the remaining barbecue sauce over the top of each loaf. Return the pan to the oven for 10 more minutes, or until the internal temperature of one of the mini loaves reaches 165°F. (Note: If you use a regular muffin tin instead of a mini loaf pan, the cooking time may be shorter due to the smaller size of each meat loaf.)

Serve immediately with the fresh cilantro and sliced jalapeño, if you like, for a little kick.

2 teaspoons extra-virgin olive oil or olive oil spray, for greasing

½ cup almond flour crackers (I like Simple Mills)

1 pound organic ground beef (or your favorite protein)

1 pound organic ground turkey

¾ cup diced white onion

¾ cup diced yellow or red bell pepper

⅓ cup crumbled feta or cheese of your choice

¼ cup chopped scallions (white and light green parts)

1 (8-ounce) jar barbecue sauce (I prefer Primal Kitchen)

1 large pasture-raised egg, lightly beaten

2 tablespoons coconut aminos

½ small jalapeño, stemmed, seeded, and diced, optional

1 tablespoon minced garlic

1 teaspoon Kosher salt

½ teaspoon freshly ground black pepper

½ teaspoon smoked paprika

¼ cup chopped fresh cilantro, for serving

Sliced fresh jalapeño, for serving, optional

Mexican Street Tacos
with Avocado Chimichurri

We eat tacos all the time in our house. But *these* tacos, I promise you, are life altering. Not only are the chicken thighs juicy and tender, but the avocado chimichurri seals the deal. It packs so much flavor that I always have to sneak a few spoonfuls of the chimichurri as I'm making it. As for the other toppings, pick your faves, or let what's in your fridge dictate how you'll build your tacos. The truth is, this might be my favorite recipe in the whole book!

Serves 2

Make the chimichurri: In a food processor or blender, purée together the cilantro, parsley, olive oil, red onion, vinegar, garlic, salt, cumin, chili flakes, and pepper until smooth. Transfer the mixture to a small bowl and refrigerate until you're ready to serve.

Make the chicken: In a small bowl, combine the cumin, chili powder, salt, garlic powder, oregano, and pepper. Lay the chicken thighs on a cutting board, and sprinkle half the spice mixture over the chicken. Coat both sides of the chicken pieces with the spices using tongs or your hands.

In a medium-sized saucepan over medium-high heat, heat the oil. Add the onions and cook, stirring, for 3 minutes. Add the chicken and sear for 2 to 3 minutes per side. Add the broth and lime juice, plus the remaining spice mixture. Cover the saucepan, bring the liquid to a boil, and reduce the heat to medium-low. Simmer, covered, for 10 minutes, until the chicken is cooked through. Remove the pan from the heat and transfer the chicken to a plate. Use two forks to shred the chicken.

Return the chicken to the pan, and stir to combine it with the onions and cooking juices.

Assemble the tacos: Slice one end off the ear of corn to make it even. Stand the flat end of the ear on a cutting board, holding the other end. Using a chef's knife, carefully slice along the length of the ear between the kernels and the cob.

For the Avocado Chimichurri

½ cup packed fresh cilantro leaves

½ cup packed fresh parsley leaves

⅓ cup extra-virgin olive oil

3 tablespoons chopped red onion

2 tablespoons red wine vinegar

1 garlic clove, minced

½ teaspoon sea salt

¼ teaspoon ground cumin

Pinch of red chili flakes

Freshly ground black pepper, to taste

¾ of an avocado, cubed

For the Chicken

1 teaspoon ground cumin

1 teaspoon chili powder

1 teaspoon sea salt

½ teaspoon garlic powder

½ teaspoon dried oregano

½ teaspoon freshly ground black pepper

4 boneless, skinless organic chicken thighs (or sub chicken breasts)

2 tablespoons avocado oil or extra-virgin olive oil

½ red onion, sliced

1 cup organic chicken bone broth

Juice of ½ lime

Try to get as much of the flesh as possible without getting too much of the tough bits closer to the cob. Once all the kernels are removed, place them in a medium skillet with the oil, and cook on medium to high heat for 8 to 10 minutes or until they begin to char. Toss lightly. Set aside.

In a medium-sized bowl, toss ¼ cup of the chimichurri with the avocado cubes. (The remaining chimichurri will keep for up to five days in an airtight container in the fridge.)

Build the tacos with the warm tortillas, shredded chicken, and avocado chimichurri, and top with any combination of corn, cabbage, cilantro, onion, cheese, and jalapeño. Serve with lime wedges.

For the Tacos

½ cup seared corn kernels, or 1 ear of corn, shucked (see instructions)

1 tablespoon avocado oil or extra-virgin olive oil

6 corn or grain-free tortillas, warmed (I like Siete)

1 cup shredded cabbage (any variety)

½ cup chopped fresh cilantro

¼ cup minced red onion

¼ cup cotija cheese or cheese of your choice

1 small jalapeño, stemmed, seeded, and thinly sliced, optional

Lime wedges

Creamy Tuscan Chicken Pesto Pasta

I learned how to make my own pesto in college, right around the time I started my @rachaelsgoodeats Instagram account. I discovered that you can essentially add whatever kinds of nuts and seeds you like and also keep this classic Italian sauce dairy-free by sprinkling in some nutritional yeast (which happens to be rich in B vitamins) in place of the traditional Parmesan or pecorino cheese. Walnut pesto is one of my favorites. It packs a ton of rich flavor, not to mention including a good dose of anti-inflammatory antioxidants and omega-3s from both the walnuts and the extra-virgin olive oil. This pesto is home cooking comfort at its finest: it stands alone as a pasta sauce or sandwich spread and can transform soup, roasted vegetables, fish, or, in this case, chicken.

Serves 4

Make the pesto (I highly suggest doubling it; it lasts up to seven days in the fridge): In a food processor, process all the pesto ingredients until smooth. Leave at room temperature until ready to serve.

Make the pasta: Cook the pasta according to the package directions, drain, and set aside.

While the pasta is cooking, prepare the chicken. Place the breasts on a cutting board, cover them with a sheet of parchment paper, and pound them lightly with a meat mallet or rolling pin until they're about ¼ inch thick throughout. Cut them into 1-inch-wide strips.

In a large skillet over medium heat, heat the oil for 1 minute, until hot but not smoking. Add the chicken, sun-dried tomatoes, salt, and pepper, and cook for 5 to 6 minutes, until the chicken is no longer pink. Add the artichokes and asparagus and cook, stirring, for another 3 to 4 minutes. Add the cooked pasta, the entire batch of pesto, and the coconut milk, and carefully toss and stir to coat. Cover and cook for another 5 minutes.

Top the pasta with the chopped fresh basil and red chili flakes and serve.

For the Walnut Pesto

- 2 cups packed fresh basil leaves
- ⅓ cup extra-virgin olive oil
- ⅓ cup walnuts
- 2 large garlic cloves, peeled
- 1 tablespoon fresh lemon juice
- 1 tablespoon nutritional yeast
- ½ teaspoon sea salt
- ¼ teaspoon freshly ground black pepper

For the Pasta

- 1¾ cup uncooked brown rice penne
- 2 boneless, skinless organic chicken breasts or 4 chicken tenders
- 1 tablespoon avocado oil or extra-virgin olive oil
- ¼ cup sun-dried tomatoes, finely chopped
- ½ teaspoon sea salt and ¼ teaspoon freshly ground black pepper
- ¾ cup jarred artichoke hearts in water, drained and roughly chopped
- 1½ cups chopped fresh asparagus, cut in 1-inch pieces
- ½ cup plain unsweetened almond or coconut milk
- ¼ cup packed fresh basil leaves, roughly chopped, for serving
- Red chili flakes, for serving

Mediterranean Mushroom Pan-Seared Cod

I pull out this recipe whenever I'm craving flaky white fish and fresh, herbaceous flavor. The nourishing combination of bone broth, ghee, and veggies feels like it requires hours of loving preparation, but in fact it barely takes any time to come together. Serve this with roasted veggies and potatoes, or stir some cooked pasta right into the pan with the fish.

Serves 2

In a large skillet over medium heat, heat the oil for 1 minute. Season the cod with the garlic powder, salt, and pepper. Carefully lay the fish in the hot oil, and sear for about 2 minutes per side. Transfer the fish to a plate and set aside.

Add the mushrooms, tomatoes, and shallot to the same pan, and cook, stirring, until the shallot begins to soften, 2 to 3 minutes. Return the cod to the pan, laying it on top of the vegetables. Add the broth, basil, capers, and ghee, and squeeze the juice from half a lemon over the fish. Season with salt and pepper, cover the pan, and reduce the heat to low. Cook for 4 to 6 minutes, just until the cod becomes flaky.

Thinly slice the remaining lemon half. Divide the fish between shallow bowls and spoon the broth over the fish. Surround the cod with the vegetables and serve with the lemon slices.

- 2 tablespoons extra-virgin olive oil
- 2 (6-ounce) wild-caught cod filets, thawed if frozen
- ¼ teaspoon garlic powder
- ½ teaspoon sea salt and ¼ teaspoon freshly ground black pepper
- 3 cups white mushrooms, sliced
- 1 cup cherry tomatoes, halved
- 2 tablespoons chopped shallot
- ½ cup organic chicken bone broth
- ½ cup chopped fresh basil leaves
- 2 tablespoons capers, drained
- 2 tablespoons ghee
- 1 lemon, halved

Pistachio-Crusted Fish Tacos

It was hard to keep the taco situation under control in this book. (I mean, *I* would be into 75 recipes for tacos. . . .) These pistachio-crusted fish tacos made the cut. They're simple to prepare and they're insanely delicious. The breading makes the fish ultra-crisp and tasty; I use the same basic process whenever I cook crispy chicken tenders or chicken nuggets and just switch up the seasonings. These are perfect for your next Taco Tuesday.

Serves 2

Make the guacamole: In a medium bowl, combine all the guacamole ingredients, mashing with a fork to your desired consistency. Taste and adjust the seasonings, adding more lime juice, salt, or pepper as needed. Set aside.

Make the fish: Place the pistachios in a food processor, and pulse two or three times, just until there is a mixture of larger and finer pieces. Transfer the nuts to a deep bowl, and add the ground flaxseed, paprika, chili powder, garlic powder, and salt. Mix well and set aside.

In a separate deep bowl, whisk the egg.

Dip a piece of the cod into the egg wash to coat, then place the fish in the pistachio mixture, pressing down gently on each side so the breading completely coats the outside of the fish. Transfer the fish to a plate, and repeat with the remaining pieces.

In a medium-sized skillet over medium heat, heat the oil. Working in batches if necessary, add the fish and cook for 4 to 5 minutes per side, or until the outside is golden brown and the inside is flaky.

Assemble the tacos: Place each filet in a warm tortilla, or, for smaller portions, flake some fish onto each tortilla. Top each taco with guacamole, shredded cabbage, and cilantro. Serve with lime wedges.

For the Guacamole

2 avocados, cubed

¼ cup diced red onion

¼ cup chopped fresh cilantro leaves

Juice of 1 lime, plus more as needed

½ teaspoon sea salt

Freshly ground black pepper, to taste

For the Fish

½ cup shelled unsalted pistachios

1 tablespoon ground flaxseed

¼ teaspoon paprika

¼ teaspoon chili powder

¼ teaspoon garlic powder

¼ teaspoon sea salt

1 large pasture-raised egg

2 (8-ounce) wild-caught cod filets, thawed if frozen, cut in half

3 tablespoons avocado oil, plus more if needed

For the Tacos

4 corn or grain-free tortillas, warmed (I like Siete)

Shredded purple cabbage

Chopped fresh cilantro

Lime wedges

Zucchini Lasagna

One of the things I immediately fell in love with after moving into our current home was the garden. The summer we moved in, it was already overflowing with herbs and vegetables, which inspired me to finally activate my green thumb. I came up with a handful of ways to use the bounty, including Chocolate Chip Zucchini Bread (page 214) and then my sister helped out with this lasagna, which incorporates thinly sliced zucchini instead of noodles. It's crazy how you don't even miss them here—everyone I've made it for can confirm. It hits the spot when you want a warm, cheesy, comforting meal. And, bonus, you don't need to buy Italian sausage, because for this recipe you make your own! Serve garlic bread on the side for dipping.

Serves 4

Make the meat sauce: In a large skillet over medium heat, heat the oil. Add the turkey, fennel seed, basil, oregano, garlic powder, and salt, and cook, stirring and breaking up the meat, for 8 to 10 minutes, until the meat is browned and cooked through. Add the marinara, and continue cooking and stirring for 2 minutes, or until the sauce starts to bubble. Remove the pan from the heat and set aside.

Make the lasagna: Preheat the oven to 375°F.

Using a mandoline or chef's knife, carefully slice the zucchini lengthwise into ¼-inch-thick strips. If using a knife, slice the ends off the zucchini, then lay it on its side. Slowly cut from one end to the other. Lay the zucchini strips on a baking sheet (or two sheets if necessary), and sprinkle with 1 teaspoon of the salt to draw out the extra moisture. Let the zucchini sit for 10 minutes on the baking sheet or in a colander, then pat dry with paper towels.

In a large mixing bowl, combine the ricotta, 1 cup of the mozzarella, 1 cup of the Parmesan, the egg, the remaining ½ teaspoon salt, the pepper, and the oregano. Stir well and set aside.

For the Meat Sauce

- 1 tablespoon extra-virgin olive oil
- 1 pound organic ground turkey or chicken
- 1 teaspoon fennel seeds
- ½ teaspoon dried basil
- ½ teaspoon dried oregano
- ¼ teaspoon garlic powder
- ½ teaspoon sea salt
- 1 (24-ounce) jar marinara sauce (choose one with no added sugar)

For the Lasagna

- 3 to 4 large zucchini (about 2 to 3 pounds total)
- 1½ teaspoons sea salt
- 8 ounces nondairy ricotta cheese
- 1½ cups nondairy mozzarella cheese
- 1½ cups nondairy Parmesan cheese
- 1 large pasture-raised egg, lightly beaten
- ½ teaspoon freshly ground black pepper
- ½ teaspoon dried oregano
- 3 tablespoons chopped fresh parsley leaves
- Toasted Garlic Bread (page 90), for serving, optional

(recipe continues)

In a 15 × 12 × 3-inch baking dish, use a spoon or silicone spatula to spread about ¼ cup of the meat sauce. It won't look like much; the idea is to add just a little moisture under the first layer of zucchini. Arrange about half the zucchini slices on top of the sauce in a single layer, covering the entire bottom of the pan. Spread half the ricotta mixture over the zucchini, followed by half the remaining sauce. Repeat the layers with the remaining zucchini, ricotta mixture, and sauce. Top with the remaining ½ cup mozzarella and ½ cup Parmesan.

Bake for 45 minutes, or until golden and bubbling. You can set the dish under the broiler for the last few minutes to brown the top a bit more.

Let the lasagna cool for at least 10 minutes before serving. Sprinkle fresh parsley on top and serve with garlic bread, if desired.

Chicken Pot Pie
with Thyme Crust

This isn't a quick recipe, but it's one of my most delicious—and I developed it with a lot of love. The pot pie gains so much flavor both from the flaky crust, which is flecked with fresh thyme, and from the rich, creamy sauce inside. Make this when the weather starts to cool down and you want dinner served with a side of cozy.

Serves 4 or 5

Make the crust: Pour about 1 tablespoon of the beaten egg into a small bowl, set it aside, and reserve it for the egg wash.

Place the remaining egg and the rest of the crust ingredients in a large bowl. Using an electric hand mixer, mix on high speed until a rough dough forms, about 2 minutes.

Gather and press the dough into a ball. Cover the bowl with a paper towel or plastic wrap, and chill for at least 30 minutes.

Make the filling: Bring a medium-sized saucepan of water to a boil over medium-high heat. Add the chicken breasts, cover, and reduce the heat to medium. Simmer the chicken for 10 minutes, or until cooked through. Transfer the chicken to a cutting board and cut it into bite-sized pieces. Set aside.

In a large, deep skillet over medium heat, heat the ghee. Add the celery, carrots, and potatoes and cook, stirring occasionally, for 10 minutes. Add the diced chicken, peas, sage, thyme, salt, garlic, pepper, and turmeric, and cook for 5 more minutes, stirring occasionally. Sprinkle the tapioca flour over the mixture and stir to combine. Add the chicken broth and coconut milk, stir, and continue cooking for 2 to 3 minutes, until thickened. Remove the pan from the heat and set aside.

Assemble the pie: Set a rack in the center of the oven. Preheat the oven to 400°F.

Divide the chilled dough in half. Set one of the halves aside and cover lightly with a towel or plastic while you work with the other half.

(recipe continues)

For the Crust

1 large pasture-raised egg, beaten

1½ cups almond flour

½ cup gluten-free or paleo flour, plus more for rolling (I like Bob's Red Mill)

½ cup refined coconut oil or vegan butter, chilled

1 tablespoon ice water

1 teaspoon baking soda

½ teaspoon sea salt

½ teaspoon fresh or dried thyme

For the Filling

2 boneless, skinless organic chicken breasts, each halved

2 tablespoons ghee, vegan butter, or extra-virgin olive oil

1 cup diced celery

1 cup diced carrots

1 cup diced unpeeled yellow potatoes

1 cup peas, fresh or frozen

1½ teaspoons minced fresh or dried sage

1½ teaspoons minced fresh or dried thyme

1 teaspoon sea salt

½ teaspoon minced garlic

½ teaspoon freshly ground black pepper

¼ teaspoon ground turmeric

2 tablespoons tapioca flour or arrowroot starch

2 cups organic chicken bone broth

½ cup canned full-fat coconut milk

Press the dough into the base and sides of an 8 × 8-inch square baking dish (or a 9-inch round baking dish). Don't worry if the dough doesn't cover the sides entirely; you just want the crust to form a good base and to go up the sides as much as possible.

Place the remaining dough between two sheets of lightly floured parchment paper. Using a rolling pin, roll out and shape the dough to fit over the baking dish. Try to keep the dough at least 1/8 inch thick; otherwise, it will be too fragile to transfer onto the filling. Leave the dough on the parchment paper and set aside.

Spoon the filling over the prepared crust in the baking dish, spreading evenly. Remove the top sheet of parchment paper from the rolled-out dough, and slide your hand under the bottom sheet. Gently flip the dough on top of the baking dish, and slowly pull off the parchment paper. The dough should cover the entire surface of the baking dish. Seal or crimp the edges of the dough as desired by pressing them together with your fingers or a fork. Trim away any bits of crust that hang over the outside edge of the baking dish. Brush the reserved egg wash over the top of the crust, and cut 2 or 3 slits in the center of the pie for venting steam.

Bake for about 30 minutes, until the top crust is golden brown and the chicken mixture is bubbling. Let cool for at least 5 minutes before serving.

seven

SNACKS & GATHERINGS

We've all been there: starving with *nothing* in sight to eat besides a bag of potato chips or a vending machine granola bar that might as well be a candy bar because it's overloaded with sugar. Or we get to a party, and the only food option is a heavy dip or processed mini corn dogs. Instead of playing snack roulette, set yourself up for success by making a batch of one of these nutrient-dense nibbles at the start of the week or to use as your camouflage party dish when you go to your friends'—so you don't stress when hangry hits. I've included two snack boards (savory and sweet) that are packed with all my go-to bites; you can throw them together fast the next time you're hosting or you're asked to bring something. Your friends can thank me later!

Chewy Snack Bars

Because I train so often, I need to make sure that I stay fueled throughout the day. That's why I keep a batch of these snack bars in our fridge at all times. We're completely hooked on them, and so is anyone else who tries one. They're sweetened with honey only and have a dark chocolate drizzle on top, making them both crave-worthy *and* a healthy option. Bars keep best chilled.

Makes 12 bars

1¾ cups puffed brown rice

¾ cup roughly chopped raw almonds

½ cup raw sunflower seeds

½ cup raw pumpkin seeds

¼ cup raw hempseeds

1 teaspoon ground cinnamon

½ cup smooth cashew butter

⅓ cup honey (ideally raw or local)

2 tablespoons coconut oil, melted

½ cup nondairy dark chocolate chips

½ teaspoon flaky sea salt

Line a 9 × 6 × 2-inch baking dish with parchment paper, letting any excess paper hang over the sides. Set aside.

In a large mixing bowl, toss together the puffed brown rice, almonds, sunflower seeds, pumpkin seeds, hempseeds, and cinnamon. In a smaller bowl, whisk together the cashew butter, honey, and melted coconut oil. Pour the mixture over the dry ingredients, and use a silicone spatula to combine thoroughly.

Transfer the mixture to the prepared baking dish, and press it firmly and evenly into the dish.

Place the chocolate in a small microwave-safe bowl. Microwave for 30 seconds at a time, stirring between intervals, until the chocolate is completely melted. Drizzle the chocolate over the bars, and transfer the baking dish to the refrigerator to chill for 30 minutes. Sprinkle the flaky salt over the chocolate, and return the dish to the fridge. Chill the bars until the chocolate is fully hardened, about 30 more minutes.

Use a large, sharp knife to slice the bars into roughly 4 × 1-inch pieces. Store in an airtight container in the fridge for up to two weeks, or in the freezer for up to three months.

Peanut Butter Protein Bars

I love a good grab-and-go bar, especially when I'm short on time, as does Bridger. I wanted to re-create one of his favorite protein bars, the peanut butter chocolate chip Perfect Bar. I wasn't going for an exact replica, but I did come up with something that was equally filling and hit the same peanut-butter-plus-chocolate spot. I knew I had a winner when I developed this recipe, which calls for only a handful of staple pantry ingredients. It's perfect for post-workout nutrition, curbing hunger between meals, or even satisfying an after-dinner sweet tooth.

Makes 12 bars

1½ cups almond flour

½ cup vanilla or unflavored protein powder

Pinch of sea salt

¾ cup unsweetened peanut butter

¼ cup plus 1 tablespoon honey, warmed (ideally raw or local)

3 tablespoons unsweetened almond milk

⅓ cup nondairy dark chocolate chips, plus more for topping

Line an 8 × 8-inch baking dish with parchment paper, letting any excess paper hang over the sides. Set aside.

In a large bowl, whisk together the almond flour, protein powder, and salt. In a small bowl, whisk together the peanut butter, honey, and almond milk until smooth and uniform. Pour the peanut butter mixture into the almond flour mixture, and stir to combine. Fold in the chocolate chips.

Transfer the mixture to the prepared baking dish, and press down with a silicone spatula to smooth the top. Sprinkle with additional chocolate chips, and place the dish in the freezer for 30 minutes.

Use the sides of the parchment paper to lift the mixture out of the dish and onto a cutting board. Cut into 12 bars, and store the bars in an airtight container in the fridge or freezer.

Raw AB&J Bars

Every so often, I spend at least one week without consuming any added sugar. I just *love* how a detox from extra sweets makes me feel clearheaded, well rested, and a little lighter and brighter all around (see Chapter 1 for a two-day version of the detox). I initially created these raw bars for my no-added-sugar weeks, but they're so delicious and easy to prepare that they've made their way into everyday life.

Makes 10 to 14 bars

½ cup almond flour

½ cup almond butter

4 or 5 small pitted Medjool dates, soaked in hot water for 15 minutes and drained

⅓ cup raw sunflower seeds

⅓ cup raw walnuts

⅓ cup raw pecans

¼ cup raw hempseeds, plus more for topping

¼ cup plant-based protein powder (I prefer unflavored or vanilla)

¼ cup unsweetened coconut flakes

1 teaspoon vanilla extract

½ teaspoon ground cinnamon

¾ cup freeze-dried strawberries, plus more for topping

Line an 8-inch loaf pan with parchment paper, letting the excess paper hang over the sides. Set aside.

Place all the ingredients except the freeze-dried strawberries in the bowl of a food processor. Pulse until just combined, making sure that some larger nuts remain, for more crunch.

Fill a ½-cup measure with water, and add it, 1 tablespoon at a time, to the mixture while continuing to pulse. Continue adding water, scraping down the sides of the food processor occasionally, until the mixture reaches a dough-like consistency. (You may not end up using all the water.) Add the freeze-dried strawberries, and pulse again until just combined.

Transfer the mixture to the prepared loaf pan, and use a silicone spatula to press it into an even layer. Top with more hempseeds and freeze-dried strawberries, and gently press them into the top of the mixture. Refrigerate or freeze for 2 to 3 hours, until completely hardened.

Remove the mixture from the pan by using the sides of the parchment to lift it out. Slice into 1-inch bars, and store in an airtight container in the fridge or freezer (my personal favorite) for an easy snack or dessert.

Strawberry Shortcake Bliss Balls

I used to go nuts as a kid for those strawberry shortcake ice cream bars they sell at gas stations. Little did I know that as an adult I'd be able to re-create the flavor in my own kitchen—and eat them anytime I wanted. I swear the dough tastes like cake batter, and the second you add the freeze-dried strawberries, it's legitimately strawberry shortcake. These little guys are great because they're filled with healthy fats, which play so many roles in the body, like helping to absorb vitamins (especially A, D, E, and K), supporting the immune system, and boosting cellular function.

Makes 12 to 15 bites

¾ cup almond flour

⅓ cup cashew butter

¼ cup unsweetened shredded coconut

3 pitted Medjool dates

1½ tablespoons maple syrup

1 tablespoon coconut butter, melted

1 teaspoon vanilla extract

¼ teaspoon sea salt

1 cup freeze-dried strawberries

Line a large plate or baking dish with parchment paper and set aside.

Place all the ingredients except the freeze-dried strawberries in the bowl of a food processor. Process until the mixture has a dough-like consistency. Add the freeze-dried strawberries, and pulse a few times if you want it crunchy, or pulse longer for a smoother consistency.

Using your hands, form the dough into 1-inch balls and set them on the lined plate. The dough may be crumbly; just press it together tightly as you roll it between your palms.

Let the bites set in the fridge for at least 20 minutes. Store in an airtight container in the fridge for up to one week, and in the freezer for up to one month.

Matcha Lemon Bites

Take fifteen minutes to throw these superfood bites together, and you'll always have something both healthy and delicious on hand. The citrus from the lemon really shines, turning these into a refreshing treat any time of day—even for dessert. If you're new to matcha, don't worry, I added it with a light touch to this recipe.

Makes 12 to 15 bites

Line a large plate or baking dish with parchment paper and set aside.

Place all the ingredients in the bowl of a food processor, and process until smooth.

Using your hands, form the dough into 1-inch balls and set them on the lined plate. It helps to wet your hands with cold water to keep the dough from sticking. Don't worry—they'll firm up in the refrigerator.

Let the bites set in the fridge for at least 20 minutes. Store in an airtight container in the fridge for up to one week, or in the freezer for up to one month.

1 cup raw cashews

3 tablespoons coconut butter, melted

3 tablespoons raw hempseeds

2 tablespoons pure maple syrup

2 tablespoons almond flour

2 tablespoons fresh lemon juice

2 tablespoons collagen, optional

1 teaspoon matcha powder

1 teaspoon vanilla extract

Snickers Bites

You know those commercials that say you're not yourself when you're hungry, so you should eat a Snickers? Well, here you go! This better-for-you version is going to blow your mind. Not only do they taste like a snack-size duplicate of the original, but they have very little sugar (and the sweetener that *is* called for is unrefined). Plus, the peanuts and protein powder pack a bit of a protein punch. A game changer, if you will.

Makes 12 to 14 bites

⅓ cup unsweetened peanut butter

2 pitted Medjool dates

2 tablespoons unflavored or vanilla protein powder

2 tablespoons raw cacao powder

1 tablespoon honey

1 teaspoon vanilla extract

¼ teaspoon sea salt, plus more for sprinkling

¼ cup dry-roasted or raw peanuts

Line a large plate or baking dish with parchment paper and set aside.

Place all the ingredients except the peanuts in the bowl of a food processor, and process until the mixture has a dough-like consistency. Add the peanuts and pulse just a few times, leaving some bigger nut pieces for crunch.

Using your hands, form the dough into 1-inch balls, and set them on the lined plate. Top with a sprinkle of sea salt, if desired.

Let the bites set in the fridge for at least 20 minutes. Store in an airtight container in the fridge for up to one week, or in the freezer for up to one month.

Taco Nachos
with Restaurant-Style Salsa

Anything that involves chips and salsa has my name on it. And nachos? Forget it. I go nuts for the melty cheese and taco-seasoned chicken, and when you add home-made salsa . . . I mean, come on! If you need a good app or a game-day snack, this is for you. Plus, the five-minute salsa will 100 percent make your life better (and easier).

Photograph on page 152

Serves 2 to 4

Make the nachos: Preheat the oven to 350°F.

In a medium skillet over medium heat, heat the avocado oil. Add the ground chicken, breaking it up with the back of a wooden spoon, and cook for 5 to 7 minutes, until browned. Add ½ cup water, plus the salt, cumin, oregano, chili powder, garlic powder, paprika, and chipotle powder, stir to combine, and cover. Reduce the heat to medium-low and simmer for 5 minutes, until saucy. Remove the pan from the heat and set aside.

Spread the chips in an even layer on a clean baking sheet. Top with an even layer of about half the cheese. Use a slotted spoon to layer the chicken mixture on top of the cheese, followed by the remaining cheese. Bake for 15 minutes, until the cheese is melted.

Top the nachos with the Roma tomato, bell peppers, scallions, optional cilantro and jalapeño, and red chili flakes. Serve hot with the salsa and the nondairy sour cream.

(recipe continues)

For the Nachos

1 tablespoon avocado oil

1 pound organic ground chicken

1 teaspoon sea salt

1 teaspoon ground cumin

½ teaspoon dried oregano

½ teaspoon chili powder

½ teaspoon garlic powder

¼ teaspoon paprika

¼ teaspoon chipotle powder

1 (5-ounce or so) bag tortilla chips (I like Siete)

2 cups shredded cheese of your choice (I love goat cheddar for this)

1 Roma tomato, diced

¾ cup sliced baby bell peppers

3 tablespoons sliced scallions (white and light green parts)

⅓ cup chopped fresh cilantro leaves, optional

½ jalapeño, stemmed, seeded, and thinly sliced (or leave seeds in for more heat), optional

Red chili flakes, for serving

Nondairy sour cream, for serving

Restaurant-Style Salsa

Salsa in restaurants tends to come with . . . chips. And of course you can use any extra you make here on Mexican-inspired dishes, say, the Breakfast Tostadas with "Refried" Beans (page 42). But at home you can also expand your salsa horizons: why not try a healthy dollop on Quick Broiled Asparagus (page 185), Green Bean Sauté with Sun-Dried Tomatoes and Pine Nuts (page 189), or even Avocado Egg Salad (page 61).

Makes 2 cups

Make the salsa: Place all the salsa ingredients in a blender, and blend until smooth. Taste and adjust seasonings if needed, and set aside.

For the Salsa

½ yellow onion, peeled and roughly chopped, soaked in cold water for 10 minutes and drained (to reduce some of the onion's "bite")

1 (14.5-ounce) can fire-roasted diced tomatoes (choose one with no added salt), undrained

1 cup lightly packed fresh cilantro leaves

2 garlic cloves, peeled

Juice of 1 lime

1 jalapeño, stemmed and seeded (or ½ if you want less heat)

1 teaspoon sea salt

¼ teaspoon ground cumin

Freshly ground black pepper, to taste

Roasted Nuts, Sweet and Savory

As someone who trains most days of the week, I need a lot of energy from food to keep me going, and I need to keep the food coming consistently throughout the day. As a dietitian, I always say that when you want to reach for a snack, make sure it contains some form of protein or healthy fat in order to keep you full for longer and to hold you over until your next meal. That's where these roasted nuts come in handy. Keep a jar of them in your fridge or at your desk at work so they're an easy grab. You can also put them out as a quick appetizer for guests, especially as part of a charcuterie board (or a dessert board).

Makes 4 to 5 cups

Preheat the oven to 325°F. Line a baking sheet with parchment paper and set aside.

Place all the nuts in a large bowl.

For sweet roasted nuts: Toss the nuts with the coconut flakes, coconut oil, cinnamon, vanilla, nutmeg, and salt. Spread the nut mixture on the prepared baking sheet in an even layer, and bake for 5 minutes. Use tongs to flip and stir the nuts, and return them to the oven for 5 more minutes. Let the nuts cool completely, add the goji berries, and toss to combine.

For savory roasted nuts: Toss the nuts with the avocado oil, salt, garlic powder, cumin, and cayenne, if using. Spread the nut mixture on the prepared baking sheet in an even layer, and bake for 5 minutes. Use tongs to flip and stir the nuts, and return them to the oven for 5 more minutes. Let the nuts cool completely.

Store the roasted nuts in an airtight container at room temperature for up to a few weeks. They'll keep even longer in the fridge or freezer.

Note: Get creative with the spice blends, and use whatever nuts and seeds you have in your kitchen—this is the simplest recipe to customize!

For the Base

⅓ cup raw Brazil nuts

⅓ cup raw pecans

⅓ cup raw walnuts

¼ cup raw almonds

¼ cup raw pistachios

¼ cup raw sunflower seeds

¼ cup raw pumpkin seeds

¼ cup raw cashews

For Sweet Roasted Nuts

⅓ cup unsweetened coconut flakes

2 tablespoons coconut oil, melted

½ teaspoon ground cinnamon

½ teaspoon vanilla extract

¼ teaspoon ground nutmeg

¼ teaspoon sea salt

¼ cup dried goji berries

For Savory Roasted Nuts

2 tablespoons avocado oil

½ teaspoon sea salt

¼ teaspoon garlic powder

¼ teaspoon ground cumin

Pinch of cayenne, optional

Avocado Deviled Eggs

I wanted to include a simple appetizer that you can make for any party menu, so I reached for one that appears at my own family celebrations. The star ingredient here (and in a lot of my recipes, TBH) is avocado. Sure, it's a source of the ultimate healthy fat—along with the eggs, which are also rich in brain-boosting choline—but in addition, it's the creamy component that ties all the textures and flavors together.

Makes 16 deviled egg halves

Set a large pot over high heat, fill it halfway with water, and bring to a boil. Use a large spoon to gently lower each egg into the pot. Boil the eggs uncovered for 12 minutes. Carefully transfer the eggs one at a time to an ice bath, and let them chill for 15 minutes.

In a medium bowl, stir together the avocado, pickle, lemon juice and zest, pickle juice, and salt. Set aside.

Peel the cooled eggs, and briefly run them under cold water to remove any stray pieces of shell. Cut the eggs in half lengthwise. Spoon the yolks into the bowl with the avocado mixture, mash the yolks with a fork, then combine them with the other ingredients until smooth.

Spoon some filling into each egg white half. Garnish with the radishes, chives, a sprinkle of paprika, and the cilantro or parsley, if using. Transfer the deviled eggs to a serving plate and chill for at least 30 minutes or up to 8 hours before serving.

8 large pasture-raised eggs

½ large avocado, mashed

1 to 2 tablespoons minced dill pickle

1 tablespoon fresh lemon juice plus ¼ teaspoon lemon zest

1½ teaspoons pickle juice

¾ teaspoon sea salt

Thinly sliced radishes, for garnish

Finely chopped chives, for garnish

Paprika, for garnish

Finely chopped cilantro or parsley leaves, for garnish, optional

Heirloom Tomato and Pineapple Bruschetta

The fruits and vegetables that thrive in summer are not only gorgeous and delicious but also happen to yield loads of antioxidants, vitamins, minerals, and fiber. This Italian-inspired appetizer/snack, which showcases the freshness of heirloom tomatoes, is ridiculously easy to make. I added pineapple for an extra pop of bright flavor. The topping even works great as a side salad, sans crostini.

Serves 6 to 8

Make the crostini: Preheat the oven to 400°F.

Arrange the baguette slices on a baking sheet. Brush the bread with olive oil and rub with the garlic. Bake for 5 to 6 minutes, until crisp and golden.

Make the topping: Place all the topping ingredients in a large bowl, tossing and stirring to combine. Spoon the topping on top of the crostini, and garnish with more basil. You can also serve the topping in a bowl with the crostini on the side as dippers.

Store the bruschetta topping in an airtight container in the fridge for up to three days.

For the Crostini

1 gluten-free baguette, sliced in ½-inch-thick rounds

1 tablespoon extra-virgin olive oil

1 garlic clove, peeled and halved

For the Topping

4 medium heirloom tomatoes, diced

1 cup cherry tomatoes, halved

1 yellow bell pepper, stemmed, seeded, and diced

½ cup diced fresh pineapple

½ cup fresh basil leaves, thinly sliced, plus more for garnish

¼ red onion, minced

3 garlic cloves, peeled and minced

3 tablespoons extra-virgin olive oil

1 tablespoon balsamic vinegar

1 teaspoon sea salt

Baja-Style Coconut and Lime Ceviche

Eating ceviche is like taking a mini mental vacay to a tropical paradise. It's become one of my go-to orders every time we're near the coast—particularly on our trips to Mexico. Bridger and I have taken a few cooking classes in Cabo, where they make the most incredible ceviche I've ever had, so I knew I had to create my own version to share with all of you. It's a light, super-fresh salad with a lot going for it nutritionally—I've added coconut milk to this version for an extra depth of flavor, along with fresh herbs and colorful bell peppers. I eat it by the scoopful with tortilla chips and sliced cucumbers.

Serves 2 to 4

Slice the shrimp in half lengthwise, then roughly chop each half into four small, bite-sized pieces. Stir together the shrimp, lime juice, and salt in a large bowl, making sure the shrimp are completely covered by lime juice. If they aren't, add more lime juice to cover. Chill in the fridge for 30 to 40 minutes, until the shrimp are slightly pink. (If using white fish or scallops, chill until the flesh is fully white and barely translucent.)

Add the bell peppers, radish, red onion, coconut milk, cilantro, basil, jalapeño, and red chili flakes to the shrimp. Toss gently to combine, and return the bowl to the fridge for 10 to 15 more minutes. Serve with tortilla chips and cucumber slices.

1 pound fresh wild-caught shrimp (or frozen wild-caught shrimp, thawed), peeled and deveined; or skinless, cubed halibut, other white fish, or scallops

½ cup fresh lime juice, plus more if needed

1½ teaspoons sea salt

4 baby bell peppers or ½ standard bell pepper, stemmed, seeded, and thinly sliced

1 radish, thinly sliced

⅓ cup thinly sliced red onion

¼ cup full-fat coconut milk

¼ cup roughly chopped fresh cilantro leaves

¼ cup roughly chopped fresh Thai basil leaves

½ jalapeño, stemmed, seeded, and thinly sliced

½ teaspoon red chili flakes

Tortilla chips, for serving

Sliced cucumbers, for serving

Charcuterie Board

Not only are assembled boards the ultimate way to show off your presentation skills, but you can also make them nutrient-dense enough to cover all the good-for-you bases. I find boards satisfying to put together, and once you get the hang of it, it's fun to find new combinations and themes. This is my go-to savory board. Make sure you include a variety of components like dips and spreads, fresh fruit, raw veggies, crackers, meats, and cheeses (dairy-free options are becoming a lot easier to find), extras like nuts and seeds, and garnishes such as sprigs of fresh herbs. **Photograph on page 164**

Serves 4 to 10

To assemble the board, start with the dips and spreads. Place each in an individual bowl (make sure the bowls aren't too large for the board), and distribute them evenly. Slice the fruits and veggies a few different ways, and vary the shapes of the cheese to give the board more dimension. Arrange one or two ingredients in bunches or rows across the board. Continue with the remainder of the ingredients, saving the nuts for last to fill in any gaps. Garnish with rosemary.

Dips and Spreads

1 cup Basil Artichoke Hummus (page 166)

½ cup Olive Tapenade (page 166)

¼ cup store-bought fig jam

Fruits and Veggies

1½ cups fresh berries, larger berries halved or quartered

3 fresh figs, halved

1 cup grapes

2 cups sliced Persian or English cucumber

Meats and Cheeses

1 package salami, sliced

1 log of herb chèvre

1 brick of hard goat cheese

Dry Goods and Extras

½ cup brown rice crackers

1 cup almond flour crackers

½ cup cornichons

1 package raw honeycomb

¼ cup Marcona almonds

¼ cup each dry-roasted cashews and almonds

1 cup Greek olives

½ cup pepperoncini

Fresh rosemary sprigs, for garnish

Dessert Board

We all love a sweet treat every now and then, but a full dessert board? I mean, *hello*. Heaven. In my opinion, there's always a reason to celebrate, aka a reason to whip up this board. Feel free to substitute ingredients depending on your preference and what you have in the kitchen. I always recommend including a variety of fresh fruit (use whatever is in season) for a boost of antioxidants to complement the sweets. You could even get ambitious and add some bite-sized Twix Bars (page 227) or Peanut Butter–Lover's Nutter Butters (page 223). **Photograph on page 165**

Serves 5 to 10

To assemble the board, start with the dips and spreads. Place each in an individual bowl (make sure the bowls aren't too big for the board), and distribute them evenly. Arrange one or two ingredients in bunches or rows across the board. Continue with the remainder of the ingredients, saving the nuts for last to fill any gaps. Pro tip: drizzle the apple slices with fresh lemon juice to keep them from turning brown.

Dips and Spreads

⅓ cup Better-for-You Nutella (page 29)

⅓ cup Salted Caramel Dip (page 167)

⅓ cup Coconut Whipped Cream (page 167)

Fruits

1½ cups fresh berries, larger berries halved or quartered

½ medium apple, thinly sliced

1 cup grapes

1 kiwi, sliced, either peeled or unpeeled

1 cup cherries

3 figs, halved

1 pear, thinly sliced

Dry Goods

1 cup gluten-free pretzels

1 cup dry-roasted or raw nuts, any variety (such as almonds, pistachios, pecans, cashews)

⅓ cup nondairy dark chocolate, broken into chunks

½ cup dried, unsweetened fruit, such as mango or apricots

Basil Artichoke Hummus

If hummus is on the app menu, I'm going to order it. And while classic-style hummus is great, this amped-up, herby recipe is something you will want to make for all your friends and family! It has tons of fresh flavor from the basil leaves and artichoke hearts, and it comes together in minutes.

Serves 6 to 8

Make the hummus: Place all the hummus ingredients and ⅓ cup plus 2 tablespoons water in a food processor or high-speed blender, and blend until completely smooth, 3 to 5 minutes. Set aside.

Make the topping: Spray a small skillet with the cooking spray. Set the pan over medium-high heat and add the pine nuts. Toast the nuts, tossing occasionally, until they are golden brown, just a few minutes.

Spoon the hummus into a serving bowl, and sprinkle with the toasted nuts. Drizzle the olive oil on top, and tear the basil leaves over the bowl. The hummus will keep in an airtight container in the fridge for up to four days; add the toppings just before serving.

For the Hummus

2 (15-ounce) cans chickpeas, drained and rinsed

1 cup packed fresh basil leaves

4 artichoke hearts (stored in water), drained, just short of ½ cup

⅓ cup extra-virgin olive oil

Juice of 1 lemon, plus more as needed

1½ teaspoons sea salt

1 teaspoon minced garlic

¼ teaspoon freshly ground black pepper

For the Topping

Extra-virgin olive oil spray or avocado oil cooking spray

3 tablespoons pine nuts

Extra-virgin olive oil, for drizzling

Fresh basil leaves

Olive Tapenade

When I was little, I would squeeze black olives onto my fingertips and pop them into my mouth, one after the other. In my twenties, I discovered that a better (and more elevated, let's be real) way to consume olives was as a tapenade.

Makes about 1½ cups

Place all ingredients in the bowl of a food processor, and pulse until combined, 6 to 10 times, scraping down the sides of the bowl between every few pulses. You want the tapenade to have some texture, so be careful not to pulse too long. Store in an airtight container in the fridge for up to two weeks.

1 cup pitted Kalamata olives

1 cup pitted green olives

¼ cup roughly chopped roasted red peppers

¼ cup extra-virgin olive oil

3 tablespoons chopped fresh parsley leaves

1 tablespoon jarred capers

1 tablespoon fresh lemon juice

½ teaspoon dried oregano

¼ teaspoon garlic powder or ½ teaspoon minced garlic

¼ teaspoon freshly ground black pepper

Salted Caramel Dip

I love when a recipe I've developed with nourishing ingredients ends up tasting even better than the "real" thing. *Nothing* beats this caramel dip! It's perfect to drizzle over dessert or fruit—or, my favorite way to use it, to add to a dessert board.

Makes 2 cups

5 Medjool dates

1½ cups canned full-fat coconut milk

⅓ cup coconut sugar

¼ teaspoon sea salt

Bring 2 cups water to a boil. Place the dates in a heatproof bowl, and pour the water over them. Soak the dates for 5 minutes to soften them. Drain the dates, let them cool slightly, and remove the pits.

In a high-speed blender, blend the pitted dates with the remaining ingredients until completely smooth. Serve the dip warm or chilled.

Coconut Whipped Cream

This whipped cream was one of my happy discoveries in college, when my dairy intolerance forced me to start getting creative with my own food at home. It's so tasty that I've never looked back.

Makes 1 cup

2 (13.5-ounce) cans full-fat coconut milk, chilled unopened for at least 24 hours

¼ cup monk fruit powdered sugar (or substitute organic powdered cane sugar)

2 teaspoons vanilla extract

Place a metal or glass mixing bowl and beaters from a stand or hand mixer in the freezer for 30 minutes.

Open the coconut milk, gently spoon out the hardened layer on top, and place it in the chilled mixing bowl. (You can discard the remaining liquid, reserve it for smoothies, or freeze it in an ice cube tray for future recipes.) Add the powdered monk fruit sugar and vanilla to the hardened coconut cream, and beat the mixture at high speed for 3 to 4 minutes, or until soft peaks have formed.

Store in an airtight container in the fridge for up to two days.

eight

VEGGIES & SIDES

Side dishes are a great opportunity to fit more veggies onto your plate. These recipes will help you level up from preparing the same old steamed vegetables night after night. Here you'll find dishes that are simple to make but loaded with flavor, such as Broccolini with Caramelized Shallots, and Garlic and Rosemary Hasselback Potatoes. I've also got you covered on those nights when you're in a hurry, or if you're still working on your cooking skills, by including options that take less than ten minutes. And I've made sure to add my favorite recipes for starchy sides, such as Coconut Lime Rice.

Coconut Lime Rice

This side dish is good with literally *anything*. It's packed with a vibrant, green flavor from the fresh cilantro (I'm a die-hard cilantro fan, if you couldn't tell) and bright acidity from the lime, plus it gains a unique texture from the coconut. I highly recommend serving this rice alongside Heavy Rotation Taco Bowls (page 58), Mexican Street Tacos (page 122), or One-Pan Chicken Enchilada Skillet (page 104).

Serves 2 to 4

- 1 cup uncooked jasmine rice, rinsed well
- 1 cup unsweetened full-fat coconut milk
- ⅓ cup finely shredded unsweetened coconut
- ½ teaspoon sea salt, plus more, to taste
- ¼ teaspoon freshly ground black pepper, plus more, to taste
- Zest and juice of 1 lime
- ¼ cup packed cilantro leaves, finely chopped

In a medium saucepan, stir together the rice, coconut milk, coconut, salt, pepper, and ¾ cup water. Set the pan over medium-high heat, bring to a boil, and reduce the heat to the lowest setting. Cover with a snug-fitting lid and cook for 15 minutes, or until the rice has absorbed all the liquid.

Remove the pan from the heat and set it aside, keeping it covered, to continue steaming for 5 more minutes. Fluff the rice with a fork, and stir in the lime zest and juice, cilantro, and more salt and pepper, to taste. Serve immediately.

Roasted Sweet Potatoes
with Romesco Sauce

Sweet potatoes are often my complex carb of choice because they are full of fiber, which in turn helps prevent spikes in blood sugar and keep me feeling full for hours. Oh, and they're also delicious, especially when smothered in sauce. I love making a batch of this rich, bold romesco. It's so tasty that you'll be tempted to douse your entire meal in it. Make a double batch of sauce, and store the leftovers in the fridge to drizzle over salads, grilled veggies, meat, or fish.

Serves 4

Make the sweet potatoes: Preheat the oven to 400°F. Line a baking sheet with parchment paper.

Lay the sweet potato wedges on the prepared baking sheet and spray lightly with the oil. Season with half the garlic powder, salt, and pepper. Flip the wedges and repeat with another layer of oil and the remaining garlic powder, salt, and pepper. Bake for 25 minutes, turn the sweet potatoes, and return to the oven for another 10 minutes, until they start to crisp on the edges and turn golden.

Make the romesco sauce: Place all the sauce ingredients in a food processor, and pulse for 10 to 15 seconds, or until the mixture reaches a smooth consistency.

Transfer the sweet potatoes to a serving plate and serve the romesco alongside them. Leftover romesco will keep in an airtight container for one week in the fridge.

For the Roasted Sweet Potatoes

2 medium sweet potatoes, unpeeled, each cut into 6 wedges (or 1-inch cubes)

Avocado oil cooking spray or extra-virgin olive oil cooking spray

½ teaspoon garlic powder

½ teaspoon sea salt

¼ teaspoon freshly ground black pepper

For the Romesco Sauce

1 (11-to-12-ounce) jar roasted red peppers, drained

2 Roma tomatoes, quartered

½ cup raw almonds or raw pumpkin seeds

½ cup packed fresh parsley leaves

¼ cup extra-virgin olive oil

2 garlic cloves, peeled

2 tablespoons red wine vinegar

½ teaspoon smoked paprika

½ teaspoon red chili flakes

½ teaspoon sea salt

¼ teaspoon freshly ground black pepper

Marinated Grilled Peppers and Portobello Steaks

I got an indoor grill for our kitchen a few years back because I'm pretty sure grilled food is superior, and I was desperate to be able to make it year-round. Grilling enhances the flavor of almost anything—the simpler the ingredient (chicken breast, plain zucchini, half an onion), the better. When you marinate veggies before searing them on the grill, magic happens. I especially love grilling bell peppers, which are full of vitamin C (fun fact: red bell peppers have more C than oranges), and B-vitamin-rich mushrooms.

Serves 4

3 tablespoons coconut aminos

2 tablespoons balsamic vinegar

2 tablespoons avocado oil

1 teaspoon minced garlic

½ teaspoon onion powder

½ teaspoon garlic powder

Pinch of sea salt

4 portobello mushroom caps

2 large bell peppers, stemmed, seeded, and quartered lengthwise

Finely chopped fresh chives, for garnish

In a large bowl, whisk together the coconut aminos, balsamic vinegar, avocado oil, minced garlic, onion powder, garlic powder, and salt. Add the portobello caps and pepper wedges, and toss in the marinade to coat. Let sit for 15 minutes at room temperature.

Heat a grill or grill pan to medium-high heat. Grill the mushrooms and peppers for 3 to 5 minutes per side, until tender and slightly charred with grill marks. For extra flavor, brush the veggies with additional marinade while they cook.

Top the grilled veggies with the chives and additional sea salt, if desired, and serve immediately.

Note: If you don't have a grill or a grill pan, no problem! You can still get tons of great flavor by searing the veggies in a skillet on the stovetop.

Garlic and Rosemary Hasselback Potatoes

When any kind of roasted potatoes are involved, you know it's going to be a good meal. Don't be overwhelmed by the intricate-looking knife cuts that make these potatoes Hasselback style. They're easy to do, and the method gives them more surface area for the ghee or butter to fill.

Serves 2 to 4

5 or 6 small Yukon Gold potatoes (about 3 pounds)

¼ cup melted ghee or vegan butter, or extra-virgin olive oil

2 tablespoons minced fresh rosemary

3 garlic cloves, peeled and minced

1 teaspoon flaky sea salt

½ teaspoon fresh or dried thyme leaves

Freshly ground black pepper, to taste

Preheat the oven to 425°F. Line a baking dish or baking sheet with parchment paper and set aside.

To cut Hasselback-style potatoes, grab two wooden spoons. Place the handle of each spoon snugly on each side of a potato, and cut very thin (⅛-inch) slices into the potato. The handles of the spoons will prevent you from cutting all the way through. Set the cut potatoes on the prepared baking sheet.

In a small bowl, combine the ghee and the remaining herbs and seasonings, mixing well. Brush half the mixture over the top of the potatoes to coat.

Bake for 35 minutes, then carefully brush on the remaining ghee mixture. Return the potatoes to the oven to bake for another 25 minutes, or until tender and golden brown. Let cool for 5 minutes. Serve with additional freshly ground pepper, if desired.

Sesame Broiled Bok Choy

The best way to make bok choy is by tossing it in olive oil, salt, and pepper, and cooking it under the broiler. It comes out crispy and golden on the outside, with a juicy, tender interior. I've added sesame oil and garlic powder for flavor—and *my* goodness, what goodness! Another reason to try it? Bok choy is high in vitamin C, a powerful disease-fighting antioxidant, and vitamin K, which helps to maintain strong and healthy bones.

Serves 2

2 heads baby bok choy, trimmed and halved lengthwise

Avocado oil cooking spray or extra-virgin olive oil cooking spray

1 tablespoon toasted sesame oil

½ teaspoon sea salt

¼ teaspoon garlic powder

Set a rack in the center of the oven. Preheat the broiler to high (500°F).

Lay the bok choy halves on a baking sheet cut-side up. Spray the bok choy with cooking spray, and brush on the sesame oil. Sprinkle the salt and garlic powder on top, and broil for 5 to 10 minutes, or until the leaves begin to char. Serve hot.

Garlicky Mushrooms

My mom always made mushrooms on the stovetop (she still does), and my sis and I wondered how they came out so dang good every time—juicy enough that they'd almost burst in my mouth. It wasn't until I developed this recipe that I understood how she did it. And they're still beyond good.

Serves 2 to 4

In a large skillet over medium heat, heat the oil and ghee. Add the garlic and cook for 1 minute, just until fragrant. Add the mushrooms and cook for 3 to 5 minutes, tossing occasionally. Add the broth, salt, and Italian seasoning, and reduce the heat to medium-low. Cook for another 10 minutes, stirring occasionally.

Serve immediately, topped with the fresh chives and a sprinkle of flaky salt.

1 tablespoon avocado oil or extra-virgin olive oil

1 tablespoon ghee or vegan butter

2 garlic cloves, peeled and minced

1 pound cremini mushrooms, halved

⅓ cup organic chicken broth or vegetable broth

½ teaspoon sea salt

½ teaspoon Italian seasoning

2 tablespoons chopped fresh chives

Flaky sea salt, for serving

Broccolini
with Caramelized Shallots

Broccolini is broccoli's cooler, more sophisticated cousin. It contains all the fiber, calcium, and magnesium of broccoli, but with a milder, slightly sweet taste; it looks more elegant on the plate; and I find it easier to digest. I love it seared on the grill or sautéed in a skillet with ghee, the way I present it here.

Serves 2

In a medium skillet over medium heat, heat the ghee. Add the shallot and garlic, and cook for 1 minute, until fragrant. Add the Broccolini and salt, and cook, tossing frequently, for 2 to 3 minutes. Add the broth and cover. Cook, tossing occasionally, until the Broccolini is tender, 8 to 10 minutes.

Finish the Broccolini with the chives, a sprinkle of sea salt, red chili flakes, and a squeeze of lemon.

1 tablespoon ghee or vegan butter

2 tablespoons thinly sliced shallot

2 garlic cloves, peeled and roughly chopped

1 bunch Broccolini, ends trimmed

½ teaspoon sea salt, plus more for serving

2 tablespoons organic bone broth (any variety) or water

2 tablespoons minced fresh chives, for serving

Red chili flakes, for serving

Lemon wedges, for serving

Quick Broiled Asparagus

In just ten minutes, you can get your asparagus all charred and smoky under the broiler. The fresh lemon zest gives it the right hint of brightness.

Serves 2 to 4

1 bunch asparagus, woody ends trimmed

1 tablespoon extra-virgin olive oil

Zest of ½ lemon

½ teaspoon sea salt

¼ teaspoon garlic powder

Freshly ground black pepper, to taste

Red chili flakes, to taste, optional

3 tablespoons chopped fresh chives

Set an oven rack in the center position. Preheat the broiler to high (500°F). Line a baking sheet with foil.

Lay the asparagus spears on the prepared baking sheet, and drizzle evenly with the olive oil. Season with the lemon zest, salt, garlic powder, pepper, and chili flakes, if using.

Broil for about 10 minutes, until the asparagus begins to char.

Arrange the asparagus on a serving plate, scatter the chives on top, and serve.

Mom's Famous Potato Salad

I agree that potato salad is a summer BBQ must-have, but most of the time it's heavy with mayo and, shockingly, highly inflammatory vegetable oils. While I was growing up, my mom made this incredible version that gets its creamy kick from nothing but extra-virgin olive oil (liquid gold) and spicy brown mustard. And, yes, I go back for thirds every time.

Serves 8 to 10

Place the potatoes in a large pot, and add enough water to cover. Bring to a boil over medium-high heat, and cook until tender, 15 to 20 minutes. Drain the potatoes and set aside to cool.

Peel the boiled eggs, and chop them into bite-sized pieces. Set aside.

In a large bowl, combine the pickles, olive oil, cilantro, scallions, mustard, vinegar, salt, pepper, and paprika. Add the cooked potatoes and chopped eggs, and stir to coat the potatoes and eggs thoroughly. Cover and chill for at least 2 hours.

Garnish with additional cilantro, scallions, and red chili flakes, and serve.

12 small red potatoes, unpeeled, cut into bite-sized cubes

12 large pasture-raised eggs, hard-boiled

3 medium dill pickles, finely chopped

⅓ cup extra-virgin olive oil or avocado oil

½ cup packed cilantro leaves, roughly chopped, plus more for garnish

½ cup thinly sliced scallions (white and light green parts), plus more for garnish

3 tablespoons spicy brown mustard, plus more to taste

2 tablespoons apple cider vinegar

3 teaspoons sea salt

2 teaspoons freshly ground black pepper

1 teaspoon paprika

Red chili flakes, for garnish

Green Bean Sauté
with Sun-Dried Tomatoes and Pine Nuts

These beans have been my Thanksgiving dinner contribution for years. It's the *only* green bean dish you need on the menu—and in your life—because it isn't weighed down by weird sauces or creams (ahem, green bean casserole). The sun-dried tomatoes and garlic add depth of flavor with a fresh kick. Don't wait for the holidays to make this one!

Serves 2 to 4

2 tablespoons avocado oil or extra-virgin olive oil

½ red onion, thinly sliced

1 pound green beans, trimmed

¼ cup oil-packed sun-dried tomatoes, drained and chopped

1 garlic clove, peeled and finely chopped

½ teaspoon sea salt

3 tablespoons pine nuts or sliced almonds

In a large skillet over medium heat, heat the oil. Add the onion and cook for 3 to 4 minutes, until translucent. Add the green beans, sun-dried tomatoes, garlic, and salt, and toss to combine. Cover and cook, tossing every few minutes, until the green beans are tender but still have some crunch, 10 to 12 minutes. Transfer the green beans to a serving dish and set aside.

Wipe out the skillet and place it over low heat. Add the pine nuts, and toast until just golden brown, 1 to 2 minutes. Top the green beans with the toasted nuts and serve.

Za'atar Roasted Carrots
with Tahini Dressing

There's a very narrow window for creating the most ideal roasted carrots. If they're undercooked, you don't get enough roasty flavor. If they're overcooked and mushy, ya lost me. But once you learn how to hit that window—and season them perfectly—you'll have an all-seasons side dish to serve on repeat. Please meet my Za'atar Roasted Carrots.

Serves 2 to 4

Make the dressing: In a medium-sized bowl, whisk together all the dressing ingredients plus 1 tablespoon water until smooth. Set aside.

Make the za'atar: In a small jar, combine all the za'atar ingredients, stirring well. Set aside.

Make the carrots: Preheat the oven to 400°F. Line a baking sheet with parchment paper and set aside.

In a medium-sized bowl, toss the carrots with 1 tablespoon of the avocado oil. Season with 1½ teaspoons za'atar, and toss again to coat. Spread the carrots in an even layer on the prepared baking sheet. Roast for 30 minutes, flip the carrots, and return them to the oven for another 10 to 20 minutes, until tender.

In a small skillet over medium heat, briefly heat the remaining ¼ teaspoon oil. Add the pumpkin seeds and salt, and cook, tossing frequently, until the seeds are toasted, 3 to 5 minutes.

Transfer the roasted carrots to a serving bowl and drizzle with the tahini dressing. Scatter the toasted pumpkin seeds over the carrots, top with the cilantro (if using), and serve.

For the Tahini Dressing

2 tablespoons tahini

1½ teaspoons coconut aminos

1½ teaspoons extra-virgin olive oil

1½ teaspoons fresh lemon juice

¼ teaspoon sea salt

For the Za'atar Seasoning

2 tablespoons dried thyme

2 tablespoons toasted sesame seeds

1 tablespoon ground sumac

1½ teaspoons dried oregano

½ teaspoon sea salt

For the Roasted Carrots

2 bunches carrots, washed and trimmed

1 tablespoon plus ¼ teaspoon avocado oil

1½ teaspoons za'atar seasoning

2 tablespoons raw pumpkin seeds

Pinch of sea salt

2 tablespoons freshly chopped cilantro leaves, optional

Blistered Shishito Peppers
with Smoked Salt

This might be the easiest side dish in the whole chapter, but I can assure you that the taste doesn't give away the simplicity. The secret is a dash of tamari, a gluten-free soy sauce that I like adding to Asian-inspired dishes. The zing of tamari combined with the smokiness of the salt takes the peppers to a restaurant-worthy place. Just be warned—one in every ten shishitos is spicy!

1/2 tablespoon avocado oil

1 (6-ounce) bag shishito peppers

1 tablespoon tamari

1/2 teaspoon smoked salt (such as Maldon)

Serves 2 or 3

In a medium-sized skillet over medium-high heat, heat the oil for 1 minute. Add the peppers and cook, tossing frequently, for 5 minutes. Reduce the heat to medium, add the tamari and salt, and toss to combine. Continue cooking until the peppers char nicely, another 5 minutes or so. If you like, you can cover the pan and cook for a minute more to help the peppers steam.

Serve immediately.

nine

SWEETS

There's a reason this is one of the longest chapters in the book. I love a bite of something sweet pretty much any time of day. Tell me I'm not alone! Desserts are also my favorite recipes to create, even though sometimes they take the most time to perfect. It's easy to make things that taste great when you're using refined sugar, butter, vegetable oils, and heavy cream, but the real fun (and challenge) is creating recipes that showcase just how *delicious* food can taste when you use simple, unprocessed ingredients. Many of the following recipes re-create decadent treats, one childhood favorite at a time.

Copycat Reese's Cups

Every year at Halloween, when my sister and I divided up our candy to make tradesies with each other, my Reese's Peanut Butter Cups were a *no-go*. And they are still near and dear to my heart, which is why I've re-created basically every holiday version. And get this: my variation on the classic cups is made using only six simple ingredients. Clear out some room in your freezer for a small stash— that's what we do at our house. **Photograph on page 194**

Makes 12 peanut butter cups

Make the chocolate coating: In a small saucepan over low heat, melt the chips, stirring constantly. Or use the microwave, heating the chips in a microwave-safe dish in 30-second intervals, stirring in between, until the chocolate is melted and smooth.

Place paper liners in a cupcake tin, or use an unlined silicone ice cube tray as the base. Spoon melted chocolate into each liner to cover the bottom, about 1 teaspoon per cup. Use the back of a spoon to spread the chocolate, pressing it a third of the way up the sides of the liners. Make sure the layer of chocolate on the sides isn't too thick: you need room for the peanut butter filling. Transfer the tin to the freezer for 5 minutes to allow the chocolate to harden.

Make the filling: In a medium-sized bowl, combine the peanut butter, coconut flour, maple syrup, coconut oil, and salt, and use a spatula to stir until smooth.

Remove the tin from the freezer. Scoop out a small amount of the peanut butter mixture, and use your hands to roll it into a ½-inch ball. Press it gently between your palms to create a small, flat disk. Place a disk in each chocolate cup, leaving just enough room around the outside of the disk for chocolate to fill. Repeat with the remaining filling.

Use the remaining chocolate to cover each individual cup, spreading it evenly and finishing by swirling the top of the chocolate with the back of a spoon.

For the Chocolate Coating

1¼ cup nondairy dark chocolate chips

For the Filling

⅓ cup creamy unsweetened peanut butter

3 tablespoons coconut flour, or ¼ cup almond flour

2 tablespoons pure maple syrup

1 tablespoon coconut oil, melted

Pinch of sea salt

½ teaspoon flaky sea salt, for topping

Return the tin to the freezer to harden for 10 minutes before adding a sprinkle of flaky salt. That way, the salt doesn't sink into the chocolate, and it doesn't fall right off. Store in an airtight container at room temperature for up to three days, in the fridge for up to one week, or in the freezer for up to one month.

Holiday Versions

Instead of using a cupcake tin, line a baking sheet with parchment paper and set aside. Make the peanut butter filling, and form it into whatever shape you want—Easter eggs, footballs (for the Super Bowl), hearts (Valentine's Day), Christmas trees. If you want, use silicone candy molds, which come in almost any shape you can think of. Freeze the shapes for 15 minutes, in the candy molds, if using, or on the prepared cookie sheet if you've formed them by hand. While they chill, melt the chocolate. Remove the peanut butter shapes from the freezer. If using a candy mold, remove the shapes from the mold and place them on the prepared baking sheet. Use two forks to dip each shape into the melted chocolate. Return the chocolate-covered shapes to the parchment paper, and chill until the chocolate has hardened, about 30 minutes.

Paleo Almond Butter Fudge

In case you're new(ish) to healthier dessert recipes, I can assure you that this fudge, even though it consists of only five ingredients, will convert you completely. Of course, the chocolate–nut butter combo is irresistible, but the melt-in-your-mouth texture is next-level. I prefer keeping cut squares in the fridge, ready to go, but the fudge can also be stored in the freezer for a denser texture. Either way, make sure to keep it chilled because it'll melt after about fifteen minutes at room temp.

Makes 12 to 15 squares

1 cup nondairy dark chocolate chips

½ cup unsweetened almond butter or any nut or seed butter

2 tablespoons coconut oil

½ teaspoon vanilla extract

Flaky sea salt, for sprinkling

Line an 8½-inch loaf pan with parchment paper, allowing extra paper to drape over the edges of the pan, and set aside. Or use a silicone loaf pan.

In a small saucepan over medium heat, bring 2 inches of water to a simmer. Place the chocolate, almond butter, coconut oil, and vanilla in a medium-sized heatproof bowl, and set the bowl over the saucepan. Use a silicone spatula to stir the mixture until it's melted and combined. Or you can use the microwave, heating the mixture in 30-second intervals, stirring between, until it is melted.

Pour the chocolate mixture into the prepared pan, and smooth into an even layer. Refrigerate for 2 to 3 hours, until fully set and firm.

Lift the parchment paper to remove the fudge from the pan. Place it on a cutting board. Top the fudge with flaky salt, and cut it into small squares. Store the fudge in an airtight container in the fridge for up to two weeks or in the freezer for up to three months.

Chocolate Chip Cookie Skillet

This was one of my original Instagram recipes. It was inspired by the deep-dish cookies—or "pizookies"—available at a handful of restaurants you may know. I challenged myself to come up with a version that didn't use processed sugar, dairy, or gluten (so that I could partake). The result: one of the best desserts I've ever had. The secret is to eat it right out of the skillet and with a spoonful of vanilla-flavored coconut-milk ice cream on top. Isn't everything better that way?

Serves 4

Preheat the oven to 325°F. Lightly spray an 8-to-10-inch cast-iron skillet with cooking spray and set aside.

In a large bowl, whisk together the egg, cashew butter, coconut oil, maple syrup, nondairy milk, and vanilla until well combined. Add the almond flour, collagen peptides (if using), cinnamon, baking soda, and half the flaky salt. Gently fold the dry ingredients into the wet mixture, and stir until combined. Then gently stir in ½ cup of the chocolate.

Transfer the dough to the prepared skillet, and use a silicone spatula to smooth the top. Scatter the remaining 3 tablespoons of chocolate and the remaining flaky salt on top, and bake on the center rack of the oven for 18 to 20 minutes, or until a toothpick inserted in the center comes out clean. Switch the oven to broil on medium-low to turn the cookie a little more golden on top, 1 to 2 minutes. Watch carefully—the top can burn quickly!

Allow the cookie to cool slightly. Cut it into squares or wedges, or use a spoon to eat it right out of the skillet. Serve with vanilla-flavored coconut-milk ice cream if you want even more dessert goodness.

Tip: For individual cookies, increase the amount of almond flour by ¼ cup, and use a cookie scoop to arrange portions of dough on a parchment-lined baking sheet. Bake for 8 to 10 minutes, or until golden brown.

Coconut oil cooking spray

1 large pasture-raised egg or 1 flaxseed "egg" (1 tablespoon ground flaxseed mixed with 3 tablespoons water, left to sit for 5 minutes)

⅓ cup creamy unsweetened cashew butter or any nut or seed butter

¼ cup coconut oil, melted

3 tablespoons maple syrup or honey

1 tablespoon unsweetened nondairy milk

1 teaspoon vanilla extract

1 cup almond flour

¼ cup unflavored collagen peptides (for added protein) or 2 additional tablespoons almond flour

½ teaspoon ground cinnamon

¼ teaspoon baking soda

¼ teaspoon flaky sea salt

½ cup plus 3 tablespoons nondairy dark chocolate chips or broken-up chocolate bar

Carrot Cake Cupcakes
with Cream Cheese Frosting

When I was in high school and my mom asked me what kind of cake I'd like for my birthday, my answer seemed to always be carrot cake. So it was the obvious choice for one of my dessert makeovers. The new and improved version is another lighter option free of refined sugar, gluten, and dairy, including the cream cheese frosting, which is a shout-out to the frosting my sister, Maddie, used to make for us when we were kids.

Makes 10 cupcakes

Make the cupcakes: Preheat the oven to 350°F. Spray a cupcake tin with cooking spray or line the wells with paper liners and set aside.

In a large bowl, whisk together the eggs, nondairy milk, coconut oil, and vanilla. Sprinkle the almond flour in an even layer on top of the liquid mixture, followed by the coconut sugar, optional raisins and pecans, coconut flour, arrowroot, cinnamon, nutmeg, baking soda, cloves, and salt. Fold in the dry ingredients, and stir until just combined. Add the carrots and fold to combine.

Using a cookie scoop or a ¼-cup measure, divide the batter among 10 of the wells in the cupcake tin. Bake for 20 to 24 minutes, or until a toothpick inserted in the center of a cupcake comes out clean. Let the cupcakes cool in the pan for 25 minutes.

Make the frosting: Fit a hand mixer with the wire whip attachment. Place the powdered sugar, vegan cream cheese, vegan butter, and vanilla in a large bowl, and beat on high speed until smooth. Set the bowl in the fridge to chill for up to an hour or two. Once the cupcakes are cool, spread the frosting on the cupcakes.

The frosted cupcakes will keep in an airtight container in the refrigerator for up to five days. To make the frosting ahead of time, store it in an airtight container in the fridge for up to one week. Let it sit at room temperature for 10 to 15 minutes before spreading.

For the Cupcakes

Coconut oil cooking spray

3 large pasture-raised eggs

⅓ cup unsweetened nondairy milk or water

¼ cup coconut oil, melted, or avocado oil

1½ teaspoons vanilla extract

¾ cup almond flour

⅓ cup coconut sugar

⅓ cup raisins, optional

⅓ cup chopped raw pecans, optional

¼ cup coconut flour

1 tablespoon arrowroot starch

1 tablespoon ground cinnamon

1 teaspoon ground nutmeg

1 teaspoon baking soda

½ teaspoon ground cloves

¼ teaspoon sea salt

1½ cups shredded carrot (from about 3 to 4 medium carrots)

For the Frosting

½ cup powdered monk fruit sugar or organic powdered cane sugar

⅓ cup vegan cream cheese

¼ cup vegan butter

1 teaspoon vanilla extract

Raw Cheesecake
with Strawberries

Both my mom and Bridger are the biggest fans of plain cheesecake (they're snobs, if you will), and they always insist that cheesecake *has* to be ice cold or forget it. Challenge accepted. Not only did I come up with a cheesecake that uses just maple syrup and dates as the sweetener, but it utilizes cashews to re-create that classic creamy texture. I'd like to say it's a particularly sophisticated no-bake dessert. I know I really hit the mark with this one because my mom and Bridger haven't stopped raving about it.

Serves 8 to 10

Make the crust: Cut two 4-inch-wide strips of parchment paper, each at least 15 inches long. Spray a 9-inch round cake pan lightly with cooking oil. Make an X with the parchment strips, and lay them in the pan, creasing them to conform to the bottom and sides of the pan. This will make it easier to remove the cheesecake when it's done.

Place the cashews, dates, pecans, flaxseed, cinnamon, water, and salt in the bowl of a food processor, and pulse until the mixture has a dough-like consistency. Transfer the mixture to the prepared cake pan, and press it into an even layer using a silicone spatula. Set aside.

Make the filling: Put all the filling ingredients in a high-speed blender, and blend until smooth. Pour the mixture into the prepared crust, and place it in the freezer to set for 3 hours, or until the center is completely hardened.

Remove the cheesecake from the freezer, and let it sit at room temperature for 10 minutes. Gently pull up on the ends of the parchment paper to lift the cheesecake out of the pan. Transfer it to a serving plate.

Decorate the cake with the fresh strawberries and coconut flakes, if using, and let sit for another 10 to 20 minutes to soften before slicing.

Store, covered, in the refrigerator for up to three days, or cut into slices and store in the freezer for up to one month.

For the Crust
Coconut oil cooking spray

1 cup raw cashews

1 cup pitted Medjool dates

⅓ cup raw pecans

¼ cup ground flaxseed

¼ teaspoon ground cinnamon

¼ teaspoon sea salt

2 tablespoons water

For the Filling
1½ cups raw cashews, soaked in boiling water for 10 minutes and drained

1 cup canned unsweetened coconut cream

¼ cup fresh lemon juice

3 tablespoons maple syrup or honey

1½ tablespoons coconut oil, melted

1 teaspoon vanilla extract

For the Topping
1 cup sliced fresh strawberries

¼ cup unsweetened shredded coconut, optional

Oatmeal Chocolate Chip Cookies

Grandma's oatmeal cookies were unlike anything else when I was little, and to this day I can't resist them. Luckily, it was easy to put my own spin on them, and as a superfood bonus I like to fold in some ground flaxseed. I love using flaxseed in my desserts: thanks to its high fiber content, it's great for stabilizing blood sugar levels, and it's rich in healthy, heart-supporting oils. Win!

Makes 12 cookies

1 large pasture-raised egg

¼ cup tahini

3 tablespoons coconut oil, melted

2 tablespoons maple syrup

1 teaspoon vanilla extract

1 cup plus 3 tablespoons sprouted rolled oats (nonsprouted work too)

⅓ cup nondairy semisweet or dark chocolate chips

¼ cup almond flour

3 tablespoons coconut sugar

2 tablespoons ground flaxseed

½ teaspoon baking soda

½ teaspoon flaky sea salt, plus more for finishing

¼ teaspoon ground cinnamon

Preheat the oven to 350°F. Line a baking sheet with parchment paper and set aside.

In a large mixing bowl, whisk together the egg, tahini, coconut oil, maple syrup, and vanilla until smooth. Sprinkle the oats evenly over the wet mixture, followed by the chocolate chips, almond flour, coconut sugar, ground flaxseed, baking soda, flaky salt, and cinnamon. Fold in the dry ingredients, and stir until just combined.

Using a medium-sized cookie scoop or two oiled spoons, divide the dough evenly into 12 portions, flattening the bottom of each by scraping the scoop on the edge of the bowl. Place them 1 to 2 inches apart on the prepared baking sheet. Bake for 11 to 12 minutes, until the cookies begin to brown on the edges. Let cool on the pan, then finish the cookies with another pinch of flaky sea salt.

Mango Sticky Rice

I'll never forget the mango sticky rice I ate in Thailand when a big group of us went there for my sister's birthday a few years ago. This dish, which is native to Southeast Asia, is naturally dairy-free. Instead of cow's milk, it calls for coconut milk and coconut cream, so naturally, I ate it nearly every night we were there. It's super rich and creamy, sweetened only with maple syrup, and the fresh mango on top is literally *everything*. When Bridger and I were at the airport to return home from Thailand, we got two orders of mango sticky rice because we knew we'd miss it. With this recipe, now *you* won't have to!

Serves 2

1¼ cups plus 3 tablespoons canned, unsweetened coconut cream

½ cup uncooked jasmine or white rice

3 tablespoons maple syrup

Pinch of sea salt

1 teaspoon brown rice flour

1 medium mango, any variety, chilled

In a small saucepan over medium-high heat, stir together 1¼ cups of the coconut cream, the rice, 2 tablespoons of the maple syrup, and the salt. Bring to a boil, stir again, and cover. Reduce the heat to a simmer and cook for 12 to 15 minutes, stirring occasionally, until the rice has absorbed all the liquid.

Using a vegetable peeler, peel half of the chilled mango. Working as closely as you can to the large oval, pit in the center, slice off a large section of the mango from top to bottom. Thinly slice the section widthwise.

Divide the cooked rice between bowls, and top with the sliced mango.

In the same saucepan over low heat, stir together the remaining 3 tablespoons coconut cream and the remaining 1 tablespoon maple syrup. Whisk in the brown rice flour to thicken the sauce, working out any clumps. Cook gently until the sauce is smooth and warmed through. Drizzle the sauce over the mango and rice, and serve warm or at room temperature.

Paleo Apple Crisp

When it's your turn to make a dessert for the holidays, *this* is the one to bring. It's a crowd-pleaser, plus it has the best crumble topping, which is truly great on its own. I'm confident you will love this recipe; just make sure you leave room for dessert!

Serves 4 to 6

Make the filling: In a large bowl, toss together all the filling ingredients. Transfer the mixture to an 8 × 8-inch baking dish, or spoon it into individual ramekins, and set aside.

Make the topping: Preheat the oven to 350°F.

Place all the topping ingredients in the bowl of a food processor, and pulse until crumbly. Top the apples with the mixture in a thick, even layer.

Bake for 40 minutes. Top the baking dish with foil and continue baking for another 10 minutes.

Serve hot with vanilla-flavored coconut-milk ice cream, if you like.

For the Filling

4 to 5 medium apples (any variety), peeled, cored, and thinly sliced

3 tablespoons maple syrup

2 tablespoons coconut oil, melted

1 tablespoon arrowroot starch

Juice of ½ lemon

2 teaspoons ground cinnamon

1 teaspoon vanilla extract

¼ teaspoon ground nutmeg

For the Crumble Topping

½ cup almond flour

½ cup raw pecans

⅓ cup unsweetened coconut flakes

3 tablespoons raw pumpkin seeds

3 tablespoons ground flaxseed

3 tablespoons coconut oil, melted

2 tablespoons maple syrup

1 teaspoon ground cinnamon

¼ teaspoon ground nutmeg

¼ teaspoon ground ginger

Pinch of sea salt

Coconut-milk vanilla-flavored ice cream, for serving, optional

Coconut Raspberry Chia Pops

Normally, store-bought pops are filled with the craziest ingredients. Not these! With only six whole-food ingredients, they will become your BFF on hot summer days. The chia seeds bring a little pop of fiber, omega-3s, and antioxidants. I'm down! Plus, you can get creative with different fruity flavors in place of raspberry—like blended mango and pear, pineapple and lime, or watermelon and strawberry. If only I had bought a Popsicle mold sooner!

Makes 8 to 12 pops

1 (13.5-ounce) can full-fat unsweetened coconut milk

3 tablespoons honey (ideally raw or local)

1 tablespoon chia seeds

½ teaspoon vanilla extract

1½ teaspoons lemon juice, optional

1 cup raspberries, fresh or frozen and thawed

In a high-speed blender, blend the coconut milk, honey, chia seeds, vanilla, and lemon juice, if using, until completely smooth. Let the mixture sit for 10 minutes to allow the chia seeds to slightly thicken the liquid.

In a medium bowl, mash the raspberries with a fork until smooth.

Divide the coconut mixture evenly between Popsicle molds, followed by the mashed raspberries. Use a long skewer to swirl the mixture and the fruit together to create a marbled appearance. Insert a Popsicle stick in the center of each, and freeze until the pops are frozen solid, 4 to 6 hours.

Chocolate Chip Zucchini Bread

This bread was a direct result of contemplating the endless supply of zucchini from our garden. My sister has always been known as the baker in the family, but after I developed this recipe (which is gluten- and dairy-free, making it, *ahem*, more difficult to execute), I'd say she might not hold that title anymore. You can feel good about eating this bread because zucchini is rich in antioxidants such as carotenoids, which can enhance your immune system.

Makes 1 loaf

2 cups shredded zucchini

2 large pasture-raised eggs

1 ripe banana, mashed

½ cup unsweetened almond butter or any nut or seed butter

¼ cup maple syrup

1 teaspoon vanilla extract

1 cup almond flour

2 tablespoons coconut sugar

1½ teaspoons ground cinnamon

1 teaspoon baking soda

½ teaspoon sea salt

⅛ teaspoon ground nutmeg

½ cup nondairy dark chocolate chips, plus more for topping

Preheat the oven to 350°F. Lay a piece of parchment paper in an 8½-inch loaf pan, allowing the edges to hang over the sides by an inch or two. Set aside.

Place the shredded zucchini in the middle of a clean kitchen towel or several layers of paper towels, and squeeze out as much liquid as you can, twisting gently (especially if using paper towels, so they don't tear). This may take a minute or two and several squeezes. Remove the zucchini from the towel, and set it aside so it continues drying.

In a large bowl, whisk together the eggs, banana, almond butter, maple syrup, and vanilla until smooth. Add the drained zucchini, and stir to combine. Sprinkle the almond flour evenly over the mixture, and repeat with the coconut sugar, cinnamon, baking soda, salt, and nutmeg. Stir gently to combine, being careful not to overmix (or your loaf may not rise properly). Gently fold in the chocolate chips.

Transfer the batter to the prepared loaf pan, and sprinkle the top with enough chocolate chips to decorate. Bake for 55 minutes, or until a toothpick inserted in the center comes out clean.

Let the loaf cool for at least 40 minutes before you dive in. It's worth the wait!

Tahini Chocolate Chunk Cookies

These are decadently rich, thanks to the creaminess of the tahini, yet they don't feel too heavy; they're like little chocolate clouds. If you're new to tahini, aka sesame seed paste (tastes so much better than what it sounds like, trust me!), the flavor is subtle and, in my opinion, makes the chocolate taste even more chocolatey. To really sell you, cacao is hormone-balancing and works to boost your serotonin levels, plus it has more antioxidants than blueberries. Top them off with flaky sea salt, always!

Makes 10 to 12 cookies

½ cup pure tahini

1 large pasture-raised egg

3 tablespoons maple syrup

3 tablespoons coconut oil, melted and cooled

1 teaspoon vanilla extract

⅓ cup raw cacao powder

½ cup nondairy semisweet or dark chocolate, coarsely chopped, or semisweet chocolate chips

2 tablespoons almond flour

¼ teaspoon baking soda

Flaky salt, as needed

Preheat the oven to 350°F. Line a baking sheet with parchment paper and set aside.

In a large bowl, whisk together the tahini, egg, maple syrup, coconut oil, and vanilla until smooth. Fold in the cacao powder 1 tablespoon at a time—this can get messy! Add ⅓ cup of the chopped chocolate, the almond flour, baking soda, and a pinch of flaky salt, and stir to combine.

Using a cookie scoop or two oiled spoons, form the dough into golf ball–sized balls. Arrange them 1 or 2 inches apart on the prepared baking sheet. Top the cookies with the remaining chocolate, and bake for 8 or 9 minutes, until the cookies have firmly set. Once they've cooled slightly (but not all the way), sprinkle more flaky salt on top of each cookie. Let them cool for at least 5 minutes before serving.

Paleo Pear Crisps

Sure, fall is amazing because of the cozy vibes and all that. But for me, it's about the pears. They're one of my favorite fruits to snack on during their peak season, usually sliced, sprinkled with cinnamon, and dipped in peanut butter. You know, for another filling-snack combo with a boost of nutrients. And then there's this sweet treat. The next time you're debating what the best fall dessert is, remember that pears have weaker cell walls than apples, meaning they cook quite a bit faster, meaning there's less time to wait before you can dig in!

Serves 2 to 4

Coconut oil cooking spray

¼ cup raw walnuts

¼ cup raw pecans

¼ cup almond flour

2 tablespoons ground flaxseed

2 tablespoons unsweetened coconut flakes

½ teaspoon ground cinnamon, plus more for sprinkling

2 tablespoons coconut oil, melted and cooled

2 tablespoons honey

½ teaspoon vanilla extract

2 ripe pears (Anjou or Bosc preferred), halved and seeded (leave the stem on one of the halves of each pear, if you wish, for a rustic appearance)

Preheat the oven to 350°F. Grease an 8 × 8-inch baking dish with cooking spray and set aside.

In a food processor, pulse together the walnuts, pecans, almond flour, ground flaxseed, coconut, and cinnamon a few times to create a mixture with a rough, crumbly texture.

In a medium-sized bowl, stir together the coconut oil, honey, and vanilla. Transfer the nut mixture to the bowl, and mix well with a silicone spatula to combine.

Lay the pear halves cut-side up in the prepared baking dish. Divide the nut topping between the pears, sprinkle with additional cinnamon, and spray once more with coconut oil. Bake for 20 minutes, until the pears are tender and the topping is golden brown and fragrant. Let cool for 5 minutes before serving.

Key Lime Tarts

Sometimes after dinner I like just a few bites of something light and sweet. It truly completes my meal in most instances. Anyone else? These individual tarts are perfect for just that; the brightness of the limes and the texture of the filling are unmatched.

Makes 4 mini tarts

Make the crust: Place all the crust ingredients in the bowl of a food processor, and pulse several times, until the mixture forms a dough-like consistency. Divide the mixture between four 10-ounce ramekins (or place it in one 9-inch pie pan), pressing it evenly into the bottom and sides of each ramekin. Set aside.

Make the filling: In a high-speed blender, blend together all the filling ingredients until completely smooth. Divide the mixture evenly between the crust-lined ramekins (or pour into the crust-lined pie pan). Cover and freeze the tarts or pie for at least 20 minutes to set. You can make this up to five days in advance and store it in the fridge.

Note: I love making these in individual ramekins, but you can also use a regular pie dish or, to get more bite-sized, use a cupcake tin. And although key limes are ideal for this recipe, you can use regular limes.

For the Crust

1¼ cup unsweetened coconut flakes

1¼ cup almond flour

2 pitted Medjool dates, soaked in hot water for 10 minutes and drained

3 tablespoons coconut oil, melted

2 tablespoons honey (ideally raw or local)

½ teaspoon vanilla extract

½ teaspoon sea salt

For the Filling

¾ cup canned unsweetened coconut milk

½ cup fresh key lime juice (from 4–5 limes)

½ cup cashews, soaked in hot water for 10 minutes and drained

½ avocado

2½ tablespoons maple syrup

1½ tablespoons arrowroot starch or tapioca flour

2 tablespoons coconut butter, melted

Superfood Chocolate Bark

If you're looking for a sweet treat that's sure to satisfy your craving, but you also want to keep it on the anti-inflammatory side of things, I suggest you try this recipe. I developed it when designing my added-sugar detox because I wanted to allow the option for a decadent, sweet treat that you could feel good about reaching for after dinner. The idea is to load the base of the bark with fresh and fun ingredients, like seasonal berries and salty nuts and seeds, so that each bite offers something new. I also include the option to add collagen peptides, giving you a yummy protein-rich option.

Makes 1 loaf pan

⅓ cup coconut oil

⅓ cup unsweetened almond butter or any nut or seed butter

¼ cup raw cacao powder

1 teaspoon vanilla extract

¼ teaspoon ground cinnamon

2 tablespoons unflavored collagen peptides, optional

1 teaspoon monk fruit sugar, optional

Toppings

3 to 4 tablespoons berries (fresh, frozen, or freeze dried)

1 to 2 tablespoons goji berries

2 tablespoons raw walnuts, pecans, almonds, macadamia nuts, or pistachios, chopped

2 tablespoons raw pumpkin seeds, sunflower seeds, hempseeds

Pinch of flaky sea salt

In a small saucepan over low heat, combine the coconut oil, nut butter, cacao powder, vanilla, cinnamon, and collagen and monk fruit sugar, if using. Heat and stir until liquid, whisk together, then remove the pan from the heat and allow the mixture to cool for 10 minutes (you still want it pourable).

Line a loaf pan with parchment paper. If you want the bark to be thick (¼ inch to ½ inch), reduce the area of the pan that will be used by placing a spice jar inside the loaf pan, laying it on its side beneath the parchment paper at one end of the pan.

Pour the cooled chocolate mixture into the prepared pan, and place it in the freezer for 15 to 20 minutes, or until almost completely hardened. This will help the toppings stick to the top of the chocolate layer rather than sinking into it.

Remove the chocolate from the freezer and add your toppings, lightly pressing them into the chocolate to embed them as needed. Return the pan to the freezer until the bark is fully hardened, 20 to 30 minutes. Remove from the freezer, and transfer the bark to a cutting board by lifting the parchment paper from the pan. Either roughly break the bark into various sizes and shapes, or slice it into 1-inch squares. Store in an airtight container in the freezer for up to two months.

Peanut Butter–Lover's Nutter Butters

If there's one packaged snack that I ate all the time growing up—after soccer games, with school lunch, or at home scavenging for food—it was Nutter Butters. I'm a peanut butter–lover through and through, so you can imagine my excitement when I made these from scratch using real ingredients. They're as good as the original! **Photograph on page 224–225**

Makes 8 to 10 sandwich cookies

Make the cookies: Preheat the oven to 350°F. Line a baking sheet with parchment paper and set aside.

In a large bowl, stir together the peanut butter, maple syrup, and vanilla until smooth. Add the almond flour and baking powder, and stir to combine, pressing out any clumps of flour.

Using your hands, roll the dough into ½-to-1-inch balls. Arrange them on the prepared baking sheet in pairs, placing the two tightly next to each other (but leaving space between the pairs). You want the dough balls in each pair to slightly overlap so the two cookies bake together to make a peanut shape. Use a fork to gently press down on each ball in one direction, then 90 degrees in the other direction, forming crisscross lines.

Bake the cookies for 10 to 14 minutes, until they're just beginning to turn golden brown at the edges. Transfer the baking sheet to a cooling rack, and allow the cookies to cool completely, at least 10 minutes.

Make the filling: In a medium-sized bowl, whisk together the peanut butter and maple syrup until smooth.

Turn one of the baked cookie pairs upside down. Spread about 1 tablespoon of the filling on the bottom of that pair, then press another cookie pair on top (the filling doesn't have to spread all the way to the edges). Repeat with the remaining filling and cookies. Serve immediately, or keep in an airtight container at room temperature for up to five days.

For the Cookies

½ cup unsweetened creamy peanut butter

¼ cup maple syrup

1 teaspoon vanilla extract

⅔ cup almond flour

½ teaspoon baking powder

For the Filling

¼ cup unsweetened creamy peanut butter

1 tablespoon maple syrup

Twix Bars

I hold my Twix Bars in high regard, primarily because they're consistently the most popular recipe on my blog. Don't be overwhelmed by the three-stage process; it's a lot easier than it looks and well worth it!

Makes 14 to 18 bars

Make the shortbread layer: Preheat the oven to 350°F. Line a 6 × 6-inch baking dish with parchment paper, letting the excess paper hang over the sides. Set aside.

In a large bowl, use a silicone spatula to combine all the shortbread ingredients, making sure no dry pockets of flour remain. Transfer the mixture to the prepared baking dish, and pack it down in an even layer.

Bake the shortbread for 10 to 12 minutes, until just golden brown. Set aside and let cool completely.

Make the caramel layer: In a medium-sized saucepan over medium-low heat, whisk together all the caramel ingredients. Heat the mixture until completely melted, whisking frequently, about 3 minutes. Remove the pan from the heat and let the mixture cool completely.

Pour the cooled caramel over the cooled shortbread base. Set the baking dish in the freezer until the caramel has hardened completely, 1 to 2 hours.

Make the chocolate layer: Place the chocolate and coconut oil in a small microwave-safe bowl. Microwave for 30 seconds at a time, stirring between intervals, until the mixture is completely liquefied.

Pour the chocolate mixture over the hardened caramel in an even layer, using a silicone spatula to smooth it out. Sprinkle the flaky salt over the chocolate, and place the dish in the freezer for another 5 to 10 minutes to harden.

Pulling up on the sides of the parchment, remove the entire slab from the dish and transfer it to a cutting board. Using a large knife, slice lengthwise into ½-inch-wide bars, then cut each long bar into thirds. It helps to warm the knife under hot water.

Store the bars in an airtight container in the freezer or refrigerator for up to one month.

For the Shortbread Layer

½ cup coconut flour

½ cup almond flour

⅓ cup coconut oil, melted

3 tablespoons honey or maple syrup, warmed

For the Caramel Layer

½ cup unsweetened almond butter or other nut or seed butter, creamy or crunchy

¼ cup coconut oil

¼ cup maple syrup

1 teaspoon vanilla extract

Pinch of sea salt

For the Chocolate Layer

2½ ounces nondairy dark chocolate, roughly chopped, or ½ cup chocolate chips

1 tablespoon coconut oil

¼ teaspoon flaky sea salt, for sprinkling

Salted Cookie Dough Bites

Not to get all nostalgic on you—even though that's kind of the theme here—but did you used to buy those little boxes of candies when you went to the movie theaters? You know, the Butterfinger Minis, Sour Patch Kids, Junior Mints, and Cookie Dough Bites? Believe it or not, I used to buy Bridger an insane amount of candy while we were dating in high school, and now it feels so wrong. Well, here's a *better* version of those chocolate-covered cookie dough bites. Indulging in these feels so right! They are best when eaten straight out of the fridge or freezer.

Makes 12 to 16 bites

⅓ cup unsweetened cashew butter or any nut or seed butter

2 tablespoons coconut oil, melted

2 tablespoons honey or maple syrup, plus more if needed

1½ teaspoons unsweetened almond milk

½ teaspoon vanilla extract

1 cup almond flour

¼ cup nondairy mini chocolate chips

Pinch of ground cinnamon

¾ cup nondairy semisweet or dark chocolate chips

Flaky salt, for sprinkling

Line two baking sheets with parchment paper and set aside.

In a large bowl, whisk together the cashew butter, coconut oil, honey, almond milk, and vanilla until smooth. Add the almond flour, mini chocolate chips, and cinnamon, and mix well.

Using your hands, roll the mixture into bite-sized pieces about 1 inch in diameter. Place the bites on one of the prepared baking sheets. Freeze them for 30 minutes to harden.

Place the chocolate chips in a small saucepan over low heat. Heat until melted, stirring constantly.

Using two forks, roll a chilled cookie dough bite in the melted chocolate, coating thoroughly. Lift the bite out of the chocolate using two forks, letting the excess chocolate drip off. Set the bite on the second prepared baking sheet. Before the chocolate hardens completely, sprinkle a bit of flaky salt on top of the bite. Repeat with the remaining cookie dough bites and melted chocolate. (Alternatively, you can leave some bites without chocolate, or drizzle the melted chocolate over the whole pan of bites instead of coating them completely.)

Immediately return the pan to the freezer to harden for 30 minutes before serving. Store the bites in an airtight container in the freezer for up to two months.

ten

DRINKS

There are so many ways to turn a drink into fuel for your body—or at least to make an indulgence somewhat less decadent. Whether it's transforming your cream-filled coffee into a Chai Latte or Matcha Latte, giving your immune system a quick boost of antioxidants with Ginger Shots, or turning your sugary after-work cocktail into a spicy, skinny variation on a margarita, these recipes have you covered all day long. Cheers!

Hot Cacao

We all have our cold-weather favorite liquid treats. One of mine is hot cocoa, especially if we're headed up to the mountains or anytime it's snowing. This variation is 100 percent an example of homemade superiority. I love swapping in cacao for cocoa powder whenever I can, since it naturally contains quite a few antioxidants and compounds that can lower your overall level of cortisol (the stress hormone).

Serves 1

1½ cups Creamy Cashew Milk (page 237) or other nondairy milk

1½ tablespoons raw cacao powder

2 teaspoons maple syrup (plus more, to taste)

¼ teaspoon vanilla extract

¼ teaspoon ground cinnamon, optional

Pinch of ground nutmeg, optional

In a small saucepan over medium heat, bring the cashew milk to a slight boil, then remove from heat. Transfer the milk to a high-speed blender, and add the remaining ingredients. If your blender cap has a removable center piece, remove it to let steam escape. If not, vent the cap slightly, and cover the blender with a kitchen towel. Blend until smooth. Taste and add more maple syrup if desired.

Note: Want a seasonal spin? Try adding a few drops of peppermint extract.

Bone Broth Latte

This beverage contains about 15 grams of protein. It also contains natural collagen, which our bodies produce but in reduced quantities as we age. Collagen, the most abundant protein found in the human body, helps make bone, muscle, skin, and tendon. Bone broth paired with the healthy fats in ghee will give you a nice recharge, especially when it's chilly outside. **Photograph on page 231**

Makes 1 serving

1½ cups organic bone broth (any variety)

½ tablespoon ghee

¼ teaspoon sea salt

¼ teaspoon ground turmeric

Pinch of garlic powder

Pinch of onion powder

Freshly ground black pepper, to taste

Rosemary sprig, for garnish, optional

In a small saucepan over medium-high heat, bring the bone broth just to a simmer. Transfer the broth to a high-speed blender, and add the ghee, salt, turmeric, garlic powder, onion powder, and black pepper to taste. If your blender cap has a removable center piece, remove it to let steam escape. If not, vent the cap slightly, and cover the blender with a kitchen towel. Blend until frothy, pour into a mug, and garnish with rosemary, if using.

Chai Latte

A chai latte is Bridger's go-to coffee shop order. We were buying them so often that I decided to create my own version, not just for the sake of our wallets but because a barista mentioned that their mix contained 26 grams of sugar per serving! I love throwing the chai spice into waffles, smoothies, and baked goods. The coconut sugar gives you the full coffee shop experience. **Photograph on page 230**

Makes 1 latte

Brew the espresso shots into a mug. Add the chai spice and coconut sugar, and whisk until the sugar is fully dissolved. Pour the warmed cashew milk over the espresso, and top with cinnamon.

1 to 2 shots espresso

1 teaspoon Chai Spice (page 33)

1 teaspoon coconut sugar

1 cup Creamy Cashew Milk (page 237) or other nondairy milk, warmed on the stove or with an electric steamer

Pinch of ground cinnamon, for serving

Lemon Ginger Elixir

If there's one thing that I can count on to put a pep in my step whenever I'm not feeling too hot, it's this cozy tea. Not only is lemon great for digestion; it's also a good source of vitamin C (which supports your immune system), and it helps soothe a sore throat. And don't even get me started on the benefits of fresh ginger, which tames inflammation while promoting healing. The raw honey is full of antioxidants and contains antibacterial and antifungal properties, in addition to lending a gentle sweetness. This drink is a wellness powerhouse.

Serves 2

Juice of 1 lemon

1-inch piece peeled fresh ginger

¾ teaspoon peeled and grated fresh ginger

⅛ teaspoon ground cinnamon

Raw manuka honey or local honey, for serving

In a medium-sized saucepan over medium-high heat, combine 3 cups water, plus the lemon juice, whole ginger, grated ginger, and cinnamon, and bring to a boil. Reduce the heat to medium-low and simmer for 10 minutes, or until the flavors are blended.

Divide the elixir between mugs, and stir in about ½ teaspoon of honey per serving.

Creamy Cashew Milk

Made with nothing but a few wholesome ingredients, this cashew milk is better than any store-bought milk. You'll love keeping a fresh batch in the fridge throughout the week for smoothies, lattes, granola, and cereal—and to form the basis of several of the recipes in this chapter. The best part about this preparation is that you don't need to strain cashew milk (unlike almond milk) if you have a high-powered blender and if you soak the cashews ahead of time. You can flavor it however you like: try adding a pinch of ground nutmeg and ground cloves around the holidays, or use it as your coffee creamer by sweetening it with dates.

Makes about 8 cups

1½ cups raw cashews

½ teaspoon vanilla bean paste or vanilla extract

¼ teaspoon ground cinnamon

¼ teaspoon sea salt

1 pitted Medjool date or splash of maple syrup, optional

In a medium-sized bowl, soak the cashews at room temperature in enough water to cover completely for at least 4 hours or up to overnight.

Drain the cashews and discard the soaking water. Place the cashews in a high-speed blender, and add 8 cups water, the vanilla, cinnamon, salt, and date, if using. Blend until completely smooth, 2 to 3 minutes.

Transfer the milk to a large jar and store in the fridge for up to five days. It's normal for the milk to separate, so make sure to shake before using.

Matcha Latte

For a good five years after college, I gave up coffee, and I relied heavily on matcha to give me my caffeine fix. Matcha is a superfood coffee alternative that delivers tons of antioxidants and calm energy, but without the crash. Unlike regular green tea, which you have to steep in water, matcha is made using the entire green tea leaf, offering more of those good catechins to help fight off free radicals in the body. You can use any milk alternative, but you won't want to have it any other way after trying it with my homemade cashew milk. So thick and creamy!

1½ cups Creamy Cashew Milk (page 237) or other nondairy milk

1 teaspoon ceremonial-grade matcha

½ teaspoon honey (ideally raw or local)

Pinch of ground cinnamon

Makes 1 latte

In a small saucepan over medium heat, heat the cashew milk until simmering. Transfer the milk to a high-speed blender, and add the matcha and honey. If your blender cap has a removable center piece, remove it to let steam escape. If not, vent the cap slightly, and cover the blender with a kitchen towel. Blend the mixture until frothy. Pour the latte into a mug and sprinkle it with cinnamon.

Variation: Iced Matcha Latte

For those times when you're in the mood for something cool.

1 teaspoon ceremonial-grade matcha

½ teaspoon honey (ideally raw or local)

Pinch of ground cinnamon

1½ cups Creamy Cashew Milk (page 237) or other nondairy milk

1 cup ice

Makes 1 latte

Using a matcha whisk or a fork, whisk the matcha powder with 1 ounce hot (175°F) water until smooth. Add the honey and cinnamon, and whisk again until smooth.

Fill a glass with the ice, add the cashew milk, and top with the matcha mixture. Stir briefly and serve.

Ginger Immunity Shots

Ginger strengthens the immune system, aids digestion, reduces the risk of heart disease, relieves nausea, and so much more. I use ginger as much as I can in my cooking, but when I'm feeling a little run-down or like I'm about to get sick, I amp up the dosage with a batch of these shots. Preparing my own not only saves me serious $$ (those tiny bottles add up when you buy them at the store) but it also means I can make them just the way I like them. I usually omit the honey, but it's a good addition if you're new to the intense flavor of ginger shots.

Makes about 15 2-ounce shots

2 medium navel oranges, peeled

Juice of 3 lemons

⅓ cup peeled and chopped fresh ginger

2 tablespoons honey, optional (ideally raw or local)

¾ teaspoon ground turmeric

A few cracks of freshly ground black pepper

Place all ingredients in a high-speed blender, add 2 cups water, and blend until smooth. Strain the mixture through a fine-mesh sieve over a large bowl. Push any trapped liquid through the sieve with the back of a spoon. (Discard the pulp, or freeze it and throw it into smoothies.)

Transfer the liquid to a jar, seal tightly, and store in the fridge for up to one week.

Margaritas Two Ways

I spent most of my young adult life avoiding tequila because it was just never my thing, but now it's one of my favorite spirits since it's so clean. It's made from the agave plant and contains zero sugar, and high-quality versions tend to leave you feeling great the following day (unlike the cheap stuff that I was first introduced to). I especially love a good spicy skinny margarita. Here are two of my favorite recipes that were inspired by the signature cocktails at our wedding in Cabo. The Pineapple Mezcalita, smoky from the mezcal, has a tropical flavor, and the Cucumber Paloma is refreshing and light.

Makes 1 cocktail

Cucumber Paloma

Place a small amount of pink salt in a shallow dish. Coat half the rim of a margarita glass with juice from the lime wedge, and dip the juice-covered part of the rim in the salt. Set aside.

In a large glass or cocktail shaker, muddle or gently crush the cucumber slices to draw out the flavor. Add ½ cup of the ice, plus the tequila, grapefruit juice, and lime juice. Mix with a spoon for 1 minute.

Add the remaining ½ cup ice to the prepared margarita glass. Use a cocktail strainer to pour the cucumber paloma over the ice. Top with the sparkling water, and garnish with the grapefruit slice, if using.

Himalayan pink sea salt

1 lime wedge

3 thin slices Persian cucumber, skin on

1 cup ice

2 ounces tequila blanco (I like Casamigos)

1 to 1½ ounces fresh grapefruit juice

Juice of ½ lime

2 ounces lime-flavored sparkling water, or substitute sparkling water and lime zest

Fresh or dehydrated grapefruit slice, for garnish, optional

Pineapple Mezcalita

Place a small amount of pink salt in a shallow dish. Coat half
the rim of a margarita glass with juice from the lime wedge,
and dip the juice-covered part of the rim in the salt. Set
aside.

In a large glass or cocktail shaker, muddle or gently crush
the cilantro and jalapeño slices together to draw out the
flavor. Add ½ cup of the ice, plus the mezcal, pineapple juice,
lemon juice, and lime juice, and stir well.

Place the remaining ½ cup ice in the prepared margarita
glass, and use a cocktail strainer to pour the mezcalita over
the ice. Garnish with more sliced jalapeño, if desired.

Himalayan pink sea salt

1 lime wedge

¼ cup fresh cilantro leaves

3 to 4 slices jalapeño, seeds
removed, plus more for
garnish, if desired

1 cup ice

2 ounces mezcal

1½ to 2 ounces fresh
pineapple juice

½ ounce fresh lemon juice

½ ounce fresh lime juice

Recipes by Category

VEGETARIAN

Twenty-Minute Paleo Granola
Homemade Cinnamon Applesauce
Banana Chai-Spice Waffles
Sweet Potato Toast Three Ways
Better-for-You Nutella
Blackberry Pecan Baked Oatmeal
for Two
Dippy Tomato Egg Skillet (skip the
sausage, or use a vegetarian
variety)
Fluffy Stovetop Oats
Breakfast Tostadas with "Refried"
Beans
Blueberry Streusel Muffins
Folded Greek Omelet
Salted Caramel Espresso Smoothie
Thin Mint Chip Smoothie
Dreamy Green Smoothie
PB&J Smoothie
Bring-You-Back-to-Life Smoothie
Avocado Egg Salad
Bridger's Favorite Salad
Greek Honeymoon Salad
Roasted Tomato Basil Soup
(skip the turkey if you want
to make the sandwich)
Chewy Snack Bars
Peanut Butter Protein Bars
Raw AB&J Bars
Strawberry Shortcake Bliss Balls
Matcha Lemon Bites
Basil Artichoke Hummus
Olive Tapenade
Roasted Nuts, Sweet and Savory
Avocado Deviled Eggs
Heirloom Tomato and Pineapple
Bruschetta
Snickers Bites
Dessert Board
Salted Caramel Dip
Coconut Whipped Cream
Coconut Lime Rice
Roasted Sweet Potatoes with
Romesco Sauce

Marinated Grilled Peppers and
Portobello Steaks
Garlic and Rosemary Hasselback
Potatoes
Sesame Broiled Bok Choy
Garlicky Mushrooms
Broccolini with Caramelized Shallots
Quick Broiled Asparagus
Mom's Famous Potato Salad
Green Bean Sauté with Sun-Dried
Tomatoes and Pine Nuts
Cucumber Sesame Salad
Za'atar Roasted Carrots with
Tahini Dressing
Blistered Shishito Peppers with
Smoked Salt
Copycat Reese's Cups
Paleo Almond Butter Fudge
Chocolate Chip Cookie Skillet
Carrot Cake Cupcakes with Cream
Cheese Frosting
Raw Cheesecake with Strawberries
Oatmeal Chocolate Chip Cookies
Mango Sticky Rice
Paleo Apple Crisp
Coconut Raspberry Chia Pops
Chocolate Chip Zucchini Bread
Tahini Chocolate Chunk Cookies
Paleo Pear Crisps
Key Lime Tarts
Peanut Butter–Lover's Nutter Butters
Twix Bars
Salted Cookie Dough Bites
Lemon Ginger Elixir
Creamy Cashew Milk
Chai Latte
Hot Cacao
Matcha Latte
Ginger Immunity Shots
Pineapple Mezcalita
Cucumber Paloma

VEGAN

Twenty-Minute Paleo Granola
Homemade Cinnamon Applesauce

Better-for-You Nutella
Salted Caramel Espresso Smoothie
Thin Mint Chip Smoothie
Dreamy Green Smoothie
PB&J Smoothie
Bring-You-Back-to-Life Smoothie
Roasted Tomato Basil Soup
(without the sandwich)
Raw AB&J Bars
Strawberry Shortcake Bliss Balls
Matcha Lemon Bites
Basil Artichoke Hummus
Olive Tapenade
Roasted Nuts, Sweet and Savory
Heirloom Tomato and Pineapple
Bruschetta
Dessert Board
Salted Caramel Dip
Coconut Whipped Cream
Coconut Lime Rice
Roasted Sweet Potatoes with
Romesco Sauce
Marinated Grilled Peppers and
Portobello Steaks
Garlic and Rosemary Hasselback
Potatoes
Sesame Broiled Bok Choy
Garlicky Mushrooms
Broccolini with Caramelized
Shallots
Quick Broiled Asparagus
Green Bean Sauté with Sun-Dried
Tomatoes and Pine Nuts
Cucumber Sesame Salad
Za'atar Roasted Carrots with Tahini
Dressing
Blistered Shishito Peppers with
Smoked Salt
Copycat Reese's Cups
Paleo Almond Butter Fudge
Chocolate Chip Cookie Skillet (use
the flaxseed "egg" option)
Raw Cheesecake with Strawberries
Oatmeal Chocolate Chip Cookies
Mango Sticky Rice

Paleo Apple Crisp
Peanut Butter–Lover's Nutter Butters
Twix Bars
Salted Cookie Dough Bites
Creamy Cashew Milk
Chai Latte
Hot Cacao
Ginger Immunity Shots
Pineapple Mezcalita
Cucumber Paloma

PALEO

(What is and isn't deemed to be part of a true "paleo" diet is subject to debate. Bear that in mind when considering making one of these recipes.)

Twenty-Minute Paleo Granola
Homemade Cinnamon Applesauce
Better-for-You Nutella
Butter Lettuce Salmon Salad
Greek Honeymoon Salad
Rich and Creamy Potato and Leek Soup
Baked Crusted Halibut
Whole-Roasted Lemon and Rosemary Chicken
One-Pan Chicken Sausage Bake
Mexican Street Tacos with Avocado Chimichurri
Mediterranean Mushroom Pan-Seared Cod
Peanut Butter Protein Bars
Raw AB&J Bars
Strawberry Shortcake Bliss Balls
Matcha Lemon Bites
Olive Tapenade
Roasted Nuts, Sweet and Savory
Avocado Deviled Eggs
Heirloom Tomato and Pineapple Bruschetta Topping (minus the bread)
Snickers Bites
Baja-Style Coconut and Lime Ceviche
Dessert Board
Salted Caramel Dip
Coconut Whipped Cream
Roasted Sweet Potatoes with Romesco Sauce

Marinated Grilled Peppers and Portobello Steaks
Garlic and Rosemary Hasselback Potatoes
Sesame Broiled Bok Choy
Garlicky Mushrooms
Broccolini with Caramelized Shallots
Quick Broiled Asparagus
Mom's Famous Potato Salad
Green Bean Sauté with Sun-Dried Tomatoes and Pine Nuts
Za'atar Roasted Carrots with Tahini Dressing
Copycat Reese's Cups
Paleo Almond Butter Fudge
Chocolate Chip Cookie Skillet
Carrot Cake Cupcakes with Cream Cheese Frosting
Raw Cheesecake with Strawberries
Paleo Apple Crisp
Chocolate Chip Zucchini Bread
Tahini Chocolate Chunk Cookies
Paleo Pear Crisps
Key Lime Tarts
Peanut Butter–Lover's Nutter Butters
Twix Bars
Salted Cookie Dough Bites
Lemon Ginger Elixir
Creamy Cashew Milk
Chai Latte
Hot Cacao
Matcha Latte
Ginger Immunity Shots
Pineapple Mezcalita
Cucumber Paloma
Bone Broth Latte

NUT-FREE

(Including coconut-free.)

Homemade Cinnamon Applesauce
Aussie Protein Brekky Bowl
Dippy Tomato Egg Skillet
Breakfast Tostadas with "Refried" Beans
Folded Greek Omelet
Heavy Rotation Taco Bowls
Chopped Antipasto Salad
Cilantro Caesar Salad
RGE Cobb

Tuna Niçoise Salad
Butter Lettuce Salmon Salad
White Bean Tuna Salad
Greek Honeymoon Salad
Chicken Noodle Bone Broth Soup
White Bean Chicken Chili
Hearty Minestrone with Toasted Garlic Bread
Goat Cheese–Stuffed Mushrooms
Sheet-Pan Sesame Salmon Rice Bowls
One-Pan Chicken Enchilada Skillet
Salmon Skewer Gyro Bowls with Tzatziki
Juicy Turkey Burgers with Caramelized Onions
One-Pan Chicken Sausage Bake
Mexican Street Tacos with Avocado Chimichurri
Mediterranean Mushroom Pan-Seared Cod
Zucchini Lasagna
Basil Artichoke Hummus
    (skip the pine nuts as a topping)
Olive Tapenade
Taco Nachos with Restaurant-Style Salsa
Avocado Deviled Eggs
Heirloom Tomato and Pineapple Bruschetta
Garlic and Rosemary Hasselback Potatoes
Sesame Broiled Bok Choy
Garlicky Mushrooms
Broccolini with Caramelized Shallots
Quick Broiled Asparagus
Mom's Famous Potato Salad
Blistered Shishito Peppers with Smoked Salt
Oatmeal Chocolate Chip Cookies
Lemon Ginger Elixir
Hot Cacao (use a nut-free nondairy milk)
Ginger Immunity Shots
Pineapple Mezcalita
Cucumber Paloma
Bone Broth Latte

Acknowledgments

I would not be here today, writing the acknowledgments section in my very own cookbook without all the people who made this possible. I'm genuinely so appreciative for all the time and effort you've shown me and this book.

Above all, I need to thank my Rachael's Good Eats family because without you, none of this would have been doable. To every person who has ever made one of my recipes, shared it with their friends, worked out with me on Instagram or IRL, and everyone in between: you are the reason I get to do what I love every day. I'm celebrating this book with YOU!

To my husband, Bridger: my biggest support system, expert recipe tester and, truthfully, the inspiration behind a lot of these recipes. The constant motivation you've shown me since our early days in high school together has pushed me to be where I am today. I couldn't imagine writing this cookbook without you. I love you, always and always.

To my mom, who taught me how to host, prep, and cook early on in life, and who showed me how to be the hardest worker in the room, I love you and appreciate every piece of advice you have ever given me. Even if it's how to help keep fresh basil alive.

To my recipe testing crew: Mel and Eden, you two single-handedly taste-tested nearly every recipe from this book, and for that, I'm forever grateful. You girls (and Derek and Jonah) are the real MVPs. Mom, Maddie, Danielle, Bridget, Claire, Megan, Dolly, and Courtney, you've all helped shape this book through your feedback, and I'm so thankful for you.

To my sister, Maddie, for being available to take any and all of my phone calls every day. You made me love food with your famous Christmas fudge, cream cheese frostings, and most important, your passion for pie. You have such an eye for all the small details in life, and I feel so lucky I get to learn from you. Thank you for being my biggest cheerleader and for being Bridger's unhealthy food BFF when we're together.

To my dad, for supporting me for as long as I can remember. Thank you for showing an interest in my healthy eating habits and workout routine—it'll always be my biggest win in life when you've taken up one of my healthy swaps or tips.

To the most epic team who made my recipes come to life through these gorgeous photos: Eva Kolenko, Emily Caneer, Glenn Jenkins, Brad Knilans, and Carrie Beyer. It was the best two weeks spent being able to watch magic happen! Eva, I will forever be obsessed with your photography. I'm honored that you shot my first book and that this was your first book in your beautiful studio. Emily, everything you touch turns to gold (that peanut butter swirl, are you kidding?!), and I learned so much watching you style the food in this book. Glenn, you were a dream to work with on-set and are truly so skilled at prop styling. Is it wrong if I want to get started on book #2 already?

To Rachel Holtzman and Chelsea Becker: you two were invaluable through it all and gave this book the finesse it needed to officially enter the world! Thank you endlessly for your hard work on this one.

To Alix, thank you for championing this book for the past few years—it's finally here! Nicole and Elizabeth, thank you so much for believing in me and my vision. You've played such a pivotal role in making this dream of mine a reality! To everyone on the St. Martin's team from editorial and design—Kelley, Michelle, and Danielle, to production, PR and marketing—Jeremy, Hannah, Michael, Kiffin, John, Erica, and Brant, and not to mention, Brigitte . . . It truly takes a village. Thank you!

And to Erin, my boss at Dixon Café in college, who allowed me to create my very own Good Eats Smoothie Bowl and include it on the menu. Your encouragement gave me confidence and showed me that my modest @rachaelsgoodeats page had potential for so much more than I ever thought it would.

Index